The
POWER
of
BIBLICAL
THINKING

The
POWER
of
BIBLICAL
THINKING

Ralph L. Keiper

Fleming H. Revell Company
Old Tappan, New Jersey

Library of Congress Cataloging in Publication Data

Keiper, Ralph L
 The power of Biblical thinking.

  1. Christian life—1960– 2. Bible—Biog-
raphy. I. Title.
BV4501.2.K417 248'.4 77-2956
ISBN 0-8007-0862-8

To my beloved wife, Nan,
who through the years
has made the art of
biblical thinking a joy
instead of a chore

Contents

Preface

THE POWER OF BIBLICAL THINKING is not a study in psychology. It is a study of the lives of some of the great characters of the Bible who had troubles with God and themselves. Moses did not want to do God's will and tried to refuse Him in a very "spiritual" way. God trapped Him to His glory. Jeremiah called God a liar. God trapped him, and as a result the prophet was glad to be called by God's name. Job wished he had died in his mother's womb. God trapped him. As a result Job knew that when he died, he would rise again to see his God face to face with great joy. How did God ensnare these and others? It may be that you need to be ready to become a victim of God's grace. These studies attempt to show you that to be one of God's captives is to become truly free.

May I take this opportunity to express my appreciation to my wife Nan who read the manuscript and helped me in its preparation for publication.

1

The Power of Godly Thinking

THE POWER OF THOUGHT is the greatest gift that man possesses. How to think is the most important thing for man to know. What man has for the goal of his life will determine the manner of his thinking. How he faces the problems of life will determine whether he is a positive thinker or a negative one, which in turn will spell his success or failure in life. Thus, it is important for man to *know himself* if he is to make a success of his life and to master the art of correct thinking.

What may be said of men in general can also be said of Christians in particular. One additional thing may be added to *know thyself.* That is *know God,* for by knowing God we come to have a true knowledge of ourselves. Since we have been created in His image and likeness, and since in the Bible—His Word—we have a record of what He has planned for us, it behooves us to know Him and to know His Word as well.

Calvin, in the beginning of his famous *Institutes of the Christian Religion,* makes this point very clear.

> Our wisdom, in so far as it ought to be deemed true solid wisdom, consists almost entirely of two parts: the knowledge of God and of ourselves. But as these are connected together with many ties, it is not easy to determine of the two which precedes, and gives birth to the other. For, in the first place no man can survey himself without forthwith turning his thoughts to the God in whom he lives and moves; because it is

perfectly obvious, that the endowments which we possess cannot possibly be from ourselves; nay, that our very being is
nothing else than subsistence in God alone. In the second
place, those blessings which unceasingly distil to us from
heaven, are like streams conducting us to the fountain. Here,
again, the infinitude of good which resides in God becomes
more apparent from our poverty. In particular, the miserable
ruin into which the revolt of the first man has plunged us,
compels us to turn our eyes upwards; not only that while
hungry and famishing that we may then ask what we want, but
being aroused by fear may learn humility. . . . Thus our feelings of ignorance, vanity, want, weakness, in short depravity
and corruption, reminds us that in the Lord, and none but He,
dwell the true light of wisdom, solid virtue, exuberant goodness. We are accordingly urged by our own evil things to consider the good things of God; and, indeed, we cannot aspire to
Him in earnest until we have begun to be displeased with ourselves.

We can see that Calvin declares that true thinking must rest in
God, the source of all virtue and wisdom. But what kind of God
must we know? He tells us that it is not the God of theory—made
from our concepts born of ignorance. Nor is He to be the God—the
abstract God—of the philosophers. The God we should know is a
God with whom we can have personal relations, a God who cares
for us, a God who calls forth our reverence and worship. Calvin
continues: "The effect of our knowledge rather ought to be, first, to
teach us reverence and fear; and secondly, to induce us, under its
guidance and teaching, to ask every good thing from Him, and,
when it is received, ascribe it to Him." Calvin maintains that a true
knowledge of God cannot lead toward our indifference to Him. A
real knowledge of God will call forth our obedience and service to
Him.

Thus, as believers in our Lord Jesus Christ, and God the Father, our first consideration in our thought life will be to know our heavenly Father and the Saviour in a clear, vital relationship in which we can come to know God's will and make His will ours. This demands that we turn to God's Word in which we have His record of how we are to live for Him. In the Scriptures we find how we may become men of God, thoroughly furnished unto all good works (*see* 2 Timothy 3:16,17). Through our knowledge of God's Word, we can see ourselves in the light of our shortcomings and the power of His Word can convict us and correct us (*see* Hebrews 4:12). This will lead us into the power of biblical thinking, as we master its art.

In our present study, we shall examine the life of Isaiah, the prophet, who began his career by seeing God in His full glory and holiness. This experience changed the life of the prophet. He saw himself as God saw him, confessed his sin, and was ready to serve his Lord.

Isaiah Sees the Lord

Isaiah was a great court prophet, and his ministry covered a period of fifty years. He was both a prophet of judgment and of comfort. He was given the task to condemn Judah for her sins and to warn her of the judgment which would befall her. But with the judgment which he proclaimed there was the mercy of God which was declared as well. If Israel would repent, God would be more than ready to receive her. Isaiah also reminded Judah of her covenant position which she had in relation to God.

In the opening chapters of his prophecy, it is possible that Isaiah, like us, took his preaching of judgment as a matter of course and even of delight. It is wonderful to judge others, especially when you are assured of your own holiness. What he said was correct. Israel and Judah were worthy of judgment. No doubt Isaiah, with all the force of an inspired man of God, "poured it on." There can be no doubt of the fact that the people resented his rebuke. The first five chapters of his prophecy state quite clearly the sad times of sin into which Judah has fallen. Over a hundred years before, the Northern Kingdom—Israel—had fallen into slavery because of her idolatry. Her evil ways trickled down into Judah and took root. Now Judah—the Southern Kingdom—is headed for the same fate as Israel. Thus, with all the energy at his command, Isaiah tried to stop Judah's headlong fall into oblivion.

During this period, Israel had a number of kings, some of whom were good, and others evil. King Uzziah was a good king and had reigned for over fifty years. Isaiah's ministry began during his reign. Upon his death, Isaiah went to the Temple and there experienced a great change in his life. He tells us:

> In the year that King Uzziah died I saw also the Lord sitting upon a throne, high and lifted up, and his train filled the temple. Above it stood the seraphims: each one had six wings; with twain he covered his face, and with twain he covered his feet, and with twain he did fly. And one cried to another, and said, Holy, holy, holy, is the LORD of hosts: the whole earth is full of his glory. And the posts of the door moved at the voice of him that cried, and the house was filled with smoke. Then said I, Woe is me! for I am undone; because I am a man of unclean lips, and I dwell in the midst of a people of unclean lips: for mine eyes have seen the King, the LORD of hosts.
>
> Isaiah 6:1–5

Isaiah describes for us here the setting of the Temple, which in turn was similar to the ancient Tabernacle. In the holiest part of the building—The Holy of Holies—was the throne of God. Upon it was the Ark of the Covenant, which contained the Law. The throne was known as the Mercy Seat, the place where the High priest met God to plead for the people. Above the Mercy Seat were the angelic symbols which accompanied God's presence.

Beholding this scene, and finding himself in God's holy presence, Isaiah is overwhelmed by the sight. No doubt he had witnessed this scene before, but this occasion was different. He became personally involved. He was having a true experience of worship, not mechanically going through a form of traditional worship. He saw himself as a sinner in the light of God's holiness. He saw himself as one with the people whom he had been judging in his messages. He discovered that he had been giving lip service to God and not life service. He realized that the message he was proclaiming was for him as well as for those to whom he was preaching.

What made the change? Isaiah saw himself in the light of God's holiness. He doubtless saw what he could be as well as what he was.

This is the beginning of biblical thinking. We shall never see its importance or master its art until we see ourselves as God sees us. And when this occurs, we come to the end of ourselves and begin our life with Him. Notice I used the term *we* begin our life with Him. There are some Christians who hold the view that we are to be nothing. Christ is to do everything for us. I do not believe this to be true. When Christ saved us, He meant us to be something—something for Him. I understand the reasoning of those who would have us to be nothing. They wish the Lord Jesus to have all the credit for our Christian living. Also they wish to avoid trying to live the Christian life through self-effort—living in the flesh—which isn't to be done. I believe that in their zeal to glorify the Saviour, they have overlooked the fact that the old "I" has been buried with Christ, and our new "I" has risen with Him (*see* Romans 6:3–5). Through the risen Christ, and by the power of the Holy Spirit, we have been given everything we need to live for Christ. *But we must do the living.* The Church of Corinth was given everything necessary to live a victorious life in Christ (*see* 1 Corinthians 1:1–9). They possessed everything they needed but refused to avail themselves of the provisions. Thus they became a disgraceful church instead of one who was living in His grace. Isaiah saw this great truth as he worshiped in the Temple, and it changed his attitude toward his ministry.

The experience of Isaiah brings to mind another problem which we should face. What is the nature of our Christian belief? I do not have in mind whether it is orthodox or not. There is no true Christian faith if it is not founded upon the Word of God. I have in mind as to whether our Chistian faith is a matter of mere mental assent or a true, vital, living, daily experience of our being new men and women in Christ Jesus. To put it another way, can the people with whom we come into contact mistake us for Jesus Christ? This should be our aim. Instead of being "nothing," we should be Xerox copies of our Lord. We have been predestinated, that we might be conformed to the image of the Son (*see* Romans 8:29). This is our high calling and we should walk worthy of it (Ephesians 4:1).

As evangelicals, many times we judge our Christian brethren who are quite formal in their Christian worship. They read their prayers, go through their exercises of ritual worship, and do not sound the note of "being born again." Could it be that we do far worse? We may not have a structured formalism as do those whom we judge, but we do have an unstructured formalism which gives the world an orthodox lip from our heads and an unorthodox life from our hearts. If I were to judge the power of the Christian Gospel by the Christians who profess to be saved, I would come to the conclusion that the Gospel has no power and the Bible is deceiving us for saying so. But I hasten to add that my faith is in the Bible and not in the lives of my fellow believers. I know what they are and who they are and what the Bible tells me I should expect from them when their faith is a mere mental assent and not a life changing conviction. When one really sees the Lord, it is a dangerous, decisive experience. When one really sees the Lord it demands a revolutionary change in one's life.

How Can We See the Lord?

We do not know exactly how Isaiah saw the Lord. What was the nature of the voices he heard? What was the nature of the vision he saw? At least for him it was a real experience which changed his life. How can we see the Lord? What voices can we hear that lead us to believe that God has spoken to us? How may we avoid being trapped by a mystical, subjective feeling that may be only a figment of our imaginations instead of a real, valid, Christian experience? God has given us a three-fold answer: the teaching of His Word, the testing of His Word, and the Holy Spirit who makes the Word of God live in our hearts. It is quite obvious that we may not have the same experience as Isaiah. We do share with him that as God spoke to him in the Temple, God can speak to us through His Word—the Scriptures.

Faith comes to us through the Word of God. "So then faith cometh by hearing, and hearing by the word of God" (Romans 10:17). How do the Scriptures give us faith? As we study the Scriptures carefully and apply them to ourselves, we can experiment with them, and when we fulfill the conditions, we can expect the predicted result. What happens then is that we discover that God's Word works. We continue the practice in our daily lives, and before we are aware of it faith is given to us as the result of taking God at His Word. We begin to experience the words of the psalmist. Speaking of God, he writes, "I will instruct thee and teach thee in the way which thou shalt go: I will guide thee with mine eye" (Psalms 32:8).

May I open a parenthesis at this point? It may be some of you who read these pages are Christian in name but not in reality. You go to church. You have heard of Christ. You know He died for the world. You read the Bible and admire its truths. And you have gripped many of its truths. Have these truths gripped you? Is God speaking to you personally as you read His Word? Have you come to Christ, and by so doing you realize that He died for you and rose

again that you might live with Him, not only in heaven, but here
and now? This is the beginning of the everlasting life which He
promises. And this life is not merely everlasting—without end—
from a quantative point of view, it is everlasting from a qualitative
point of view as well, in that life eternal has a personal dimension
which many times is overlooked. In His great High priestly prayer,
the Lord Jesus Himself defines the term "eternal life" for us.
"And this is life eternal, that they might know thee the only true
God, and Jesus Christ, whom thou hast sent" (John 17:3). The
term that he uses for the word *know* is not the knowledge of theory,
nor is it the knowledge of intuition. It is the knowledge of experience. This would indicate that the very moment we accept the Lord
Jesus Christ as our own personal Saviour, through the study of
God's Word and through the power of the Holy Spirit, we can enter
a daily fellowship with Him. What one needs to do is to heed the
words of the Gospel: "Verily, verily, I say unto you, He that hear-
eth my word, and believeth on him that sent me, hath everlasting
life, and shall not come into condemnation; but is passed from
death unto life" (John 5:24).

God does not ask us to believe Him blindly. The Saviour does
not choose to pull His rank by merely overwhelming us with His
authority. He invites us to experiment with the Word as we apply it
to our lives. "If any man will do his will, he shall know of the doctrine, whether it be of God, or whether I speak of myself" (John
7:17). The Word has the power to authenticate itself, and one of the
ways in which it does it is to give us a sharp analysis of our lives
when we expose them to its glaring light. "For the word of God is
quick, and powerful, and sharper than any twoedged sword, pierc-
ing even to the dividing asunder of soul and spirit, and of the joints
and marrow, and is a discerner of the thoughts and intents of the
heart" (Hebrews 4:12). There is an activating quality about God's
Word, which convicts us as to what we are, and should encourage
us to see that the Bible can also help us be what we should be in
God's sight.

The Confession of Isaiah

Do Christians need confession? Since we are saved and know our sins are forgiven, what have we to confess? As we return to the life of God's great prophet, there is something about confession we can learn from him which will be a help to us. Isaiah was not thinking about confession in terms of a sinner, rather he was thinking about confession in terms of a saint—a servant of God. As the court preacher surrounded with all the trappings of royalty, and at the same time quite close to the priesthood, it was possible for familiarity to breed contempt. If not that, at least it would have been easy for Isaiah to take his role as prophet for granted. But when he sees God in all His glorious holiness, and sees himself as he knows God sees him, his life changes. Along with seeing God, he sees the altar of cleansing with the burning coals glowing upon it. We hear his confession:

> Woe is me! for I am undone; because I am a man of unclean lips, and I dwell in the midst of a people of unclean lips: for mine eyes have seen the King, the LORD of hosts. Then flew one of the seraphims unto me, having a live coal in his hand, which he had taken with the tongs from off the altar: And he laid it upon my mouth, and said, Lo, this hath touched thy lips; and thine iniquity is taken away, and thy sin purged.

Isaiah 6:5–7

Many of us are in the same state Isaiah was in before his Temple experience. We too have sins which we, in a mistaken manner, feel are part of our Christian equipment. We do not become conscious of these things until some jolting experience focuses our attention on the Lord instead of ourselves. Part of this is an occupational hazard. Our approach to Bible study can be dangerous, in the sense that we look at the Bible as just another textbook, forgetting that it is the very food and drink by which our spiritual life is maintained.

Then again, our fellow believers are neither worse nor better than we, thus we accept our vices along with our virtues as par for the course in Christian living. We preach and teach as God would have us do, and live our Christian lives in the cozy comfort of our carnality.

It is interesting to note that Isaiah's jolting experience came during a time of real worship. The art of Christian worship is a lost art in many places today. With much of our modern music, we may well feel that we are in God's theatre instead of in His Temple. In our modern atmosphere of worship, one feels he should do a foxtrot with the Lord in the ballroom of heaven instead of bowing before Him in the throne room of His Temple. Doubtless modern worship as practiced by many does something for the feet and one's glands, but it does very little for the mind, the heart, and the will of man as far as godly service is concerned. Worship of our Lord should lead us into a serious commitment on our part to the doing of His will. This is what happened to Isaiah. He saw what he was and determined that he would be what God wanted him to be—a true servant of God in a world of men. After his confession, Isaiah heard the call.

Isaiah Answers God's Call

After his confession of sin and his assurance of forgiveness, Isaiah is in the position to both hear and answer the call of God to serve Him. "And I heard the voice of the Lord saying, Whom shall I send, and who will go for us? Then said I, Here am I; send me. And he said, Go, and tell this people, Hear ye indeed, but understand not; and see ye indeed, but perceive not" (Isaiah 6:8,9). Once Isaiah was free of self he was willing to serve; once he was free of self, he was willing to live for God. Not in great preaching alone, but in the daily relationships which were the larger part of his life.

He was sent to a people who would not receive his message.

They would not understand it because of their indifference, they would not receive it because of their sin. God knew this, but He would show His mercy through the message before He would exercise His judgment because of their rebellious spirit.

Some scholars feel that the experience of Isaiah as recorded in chapter six of his prophecy really happened at the beginning of his ministry. I feel, however, that since the first chapter indicates his ministry began in the reign of Uzziah (*see* 1:1), the death of the king and the worship of Isaiah as recorded would be an occasion for Isaiah to seek the Lord, especially since he could no longer rely upon the king.

Christian Living in Action

We have chosen this experience in the life of Isaiah as an introduction to our study of the power of biblical thinking because we want our study not to be one which will lead to a theory of Christian living, rather we would have our study to lead us into actual Christian living itself. We must begin with a personal experience with Jesus Christ as our Saviour and Lord, and we must be willing to study the Bible as our guide to Christian living. We can only do this by believing the Bible to be the very Word of God, given to us through the inspiration of the Holy Spirit. We must consider the Scriptures as our spiritual food and drink.

In the chapters that follow, we shall see how relevant the Scripture is to the daily life of the modern man and woman. We shall trace through the various types of thinking found in some men and women of the Bible, in order to see how they met their problems as they surrendered to God and became obedient to His Word. What the God of Abraham, Isaac, and Jacob did for Israel, we may expect to happen to us if we walk in the way of the Lord as revealed in His Word. Perhaps, as we study the art of biblical thinking, as illustrated in the lives of those who fully trusted their God, we too shall become masters of the art and come to know its power working personally in our lives. As we follow the admonition which God gave to Joshua may we experience the success in our living as did this great leader of Israel. For God had said to him:

> This book of the law shall not depart out of thy mouth; but thou shalt meditate therein day and night, that thou mayest observe to do according to all that is written therein: for then thou shalt make thy way prosperous, and then thou shalt have good success. Have not I commanded thee? Be strong and of a good courage; be not afraid, neither be thou dismayed: for the LORD thy God is with thee whithersoever thou goest.
>
> Joshua 1:8,9

2

The Power of Biblical Thinking

"MAN IS THE MOST REMARKABLE of all the creatures that live in the world. He is the only creature that lives in all climates, and makes and uses tools, creates fires, prays, talks, and destroys his own kind in wars. Through science, man has unlocked many secrets of the universe, such as the knowledge of the shape of the earth, the structure of atoms, and the composition of plants and animals.

"The main difference between man and other creatures is that only man has intellectual faculties and spiritual qualities along with physical ones. This spiritual side of man's nature is often called his *soul*. Members of most religions believe that the soul is *immortal,* or that it never dies. Belief in a home for the soul, usually called *heaven,* comes from this version of man's nature (Carleton S. Coon. "Man," *World Book*. Vol. 13, p. 94, 1975).

The world, in general, admires man for his great achievements, especially when his ascent from his simian ancestors is taken into consideration. The Bible, however, sees man as the capstone of God's creation, since he has come directly into this world from the hand of his Creator (Genesis 2:7). The psalmist speaks eloquently of man's high position:

When I consider thy heavens, the work of thy fingers, the moon and the stars, which thou hast ordained: What is man, that thou art mindful of him? and the son of man, that thou visitest him? For thou hast made him a little lower than the angels, and hast crowned him with glory and honour. Thou

23

madest him to have dominion over the works of thy hands: thou hast put all things under his feet.

Psalms 8:3–6

"A little lower than the angels"? The Hebrew text reads "a little lower than God." God had created man in his own "image and likeness" for man was to rule the earth for Him. Being created in God's image, man was made a rational, spiritual, and moral creature (*see* Genesis 1:26–28; Colossians 3:10; Ephesians 4:24). As a spiritual being, man was able to appreciate God's will for his life. As a moral being, he was able to act justly and righteously. As a rational being, he was able to know the will of God, and to be in fellowship with his fellowman. Had man obeyed God by following His moral and spiritual laws, as he has followed the natural laws of God which govern the world in which he lives, he would be doing marvelous things in the realm of the spirit as he has done in the realm of science.

Since man has rebelled against God, he has ignored the laws governing the spiritual and social life of man, to his own peril. This is the reason why we are forced to admit that man only preys on one another instead of helping one another. It would have been well with man had he followed God's admonition to Joshua:

> This book of the law shall not depart out of thy mouth; but thou shalt meditate therein day and night, that thou mayest observe to do according to all that is written therein: for then thou shalt make thy way prosperous, and then thou shalt have good success. Have not I commanded thee? Be strong and of a good courage; be not afraid, neither be thou dismayed: for the Lord thy God is with thee. Whithersoever thou goest.

Joshua 1:8,9

Had men followed the Law of God as they do their laws of science, they would have made marvelous discoveries in the inner space of the heart as they have in the outer space of the universe.

Well does Solomon write: "God hath made man upright; but they have sought out many inventions" (Ecclesiastes 7:29), or as the Hebrew word for "inventions" might let us say, "many angles." In spite of human stupidity, the Creator is appealing to His rebellious creatures to return and reason with Him. "Come now, and let us reason together saith the LORD: though your sins be as scarlet, they shall be as white as snow; though they be red like crimson, they shall be as wool" (Isaiah 1:18). As God pled with Israel, so He pleads with us today.

An Appeal for Biblical Thinking

No one knows the heart of man as does God, his Creator. Not only has He set the rules for the operation of the world, He has established the laws for society as a whole and for individual men as well. In a terse statement He reveals this truth to His ancient people Israel, "See, I have set before thee this day life and good, and death and evil . . ." (Deuteronomy 30:15). If Israel obeys His Law, they will discover the secret of a full, enriching life which will lead to a prosperity that will not only stand the tests of time, but of eternity as well. However, if God's Law is broken, Israel will know only adversity, death, and wretchedness. In the twenty-eighth chapter of Deuteronomy, God's blessings and curses are set forth, showing what they may expect from Him depending upon their conduct of obedience or rebellion. As in the physical world, so in the spiritual world; to break a law is only to be broken by it. Following the laws of his craft, a chemist can make wonderful things from the elements of his trade. To violate chemical law, however, is but to blow oneself into eternity. By ignoring God's spiritual laws, mankind's life is but a series of continuous moral, spiritual, and social explosions.

God did not create us to prey upon one another. Rather He would have us pray to Him and study His Word so that we might live together as He intended us to do. It is through the study of His

Word and our determination to think and act biblically that we can become a miracle people in a world of marvels, living godly lives among godless men.

The Proverb sets forth the first law of biblical thinking: "Keep thy heart with all diligence; for out of it are the issues of life" (Proverbs 4:23). Mankind has heart trouble in more ways than one. Physical trouble with the heart is serious, spiritual trouble with the heart is disastrous. Man separated from his Maker is lost, and is as restless as the sea (*see* Isaiah 57:20,21). Apart from God, he cannot be anything else. He is in darkness, and everything he does is to no purpose. In all his attempts to help meet the needs of his fellowman, he meets with failure. Well has Isaiah said, "To the law and to the testimony: if they speak not according to this word, it is because there is no light in them" (Isaiah 8:20). As a man thinks in his heart, so is he. Generally, when the Bible speaks of the heart it has in mind the emotional life of man. And we do not need to argue that man often does what he *feels* like doing, even though it is against his better judgment. Thus, the admonition for the guarding of our hearts. As Solomon so well knew, the heart can be deceitful, and the lips perverse. Man can be distracted from what he knows he should do by his greed and selfishness, by working against himself and his welfare man becomes his own victim (*see* Proverbs 4:24,25). From experience the wise king of old could write, "Ponder the path of thy feet, and let all thy ways be established. Turn not to the right hand nor to the left: remove thy foot from evil" (Proverbs 4:26,27).

The New Testament also encourages us to biblical thinking through the study of the Gospels and the Epistles. After coming to know the Lord as our Saviour, we are bidden by Him to come to know Him by learning of Him. "Come unto me, all ye that labour and are heavy laden, and I will give you rest. Take my yoke upon you, and learn of me; for I am meek and lowly in heart: and ye shall find rest unto your souls. For my yoke is easy, and my burden is light" (Matthew 11:28–30). The Christian is to "learn" of

Christ. This involves two things: surrender to Him and studying the Word to learn of Him. The term *learn* in the Greek text gives us our word *mathematics,* which leads to a pun of grace. What our Lord is telling us is to "figure me out—learn of me," and by doing this, we can become at home with our Lord. And such a knowledge of our Saviour will cause us to keep our hearts "with all diligence."

In His Sermon on the Mount, our Divine Lord again emphasizes the necessity of knowing God's Word if we are to be the people God intends us to be. He reaffirms His admonition by pointing out that man is too concerned with material things which lead to greed and selfishness. Man cannot build a world with bad bricks. He cannot make a better society if he himself is sick. Thus, our Lord puts first things first. Man must be right with God before he will be just with his fellows.

> Therefore take no thought, saying, What shall we eat? or, What shall we drink? or, Wherewithal shall we be clothed? (For after all these things do the Gentiles seek:) for your heavenly Father knoweth that ye have need of all these things. But seek ye first the kingdom of God, and his righteousness; and all these things shall be added unto you.
>
> Matthew 6:31–33

Sometime ago, I visited a home. My host said to me, "Ralph, I want to invite some businessmen to lunch and I want you to tell them why they should come to know our Lord. I do not want you to use theological terms which they will not understand. Be practical, make the truth relevant!" This was a tall order, and I only had about three hours to prepare for the meeting. I thought, "Should I use philosophy? What could I say about economics or the habits of society?" Thinking that God would only bless His Word and not my secular musings, I searched the Scriptures for a passage which might appeal to businessmen.

After enjoying a delicious meal, the conversation began with the men discussing world conditions. From their discussion I gathered that the restlessness in the world, the greed of men, and the lack of happiness troubled them the most. My host, breaking into the conversation, asked me what the Bible had to say concerning these matters, and what the remedy might be from God's Word. Thinking of the words of our Saviour, I thought of Paul's confirmation as recorded in the Epistle to the Romans: "For the kingdom of God is not meat and drink; but righteousness, peace, and joy in the Holy Ghost" (Romans 14:17). "When material things are put first," I said, "and God is forgotten, there will be no justice, no peace, and no happiness in the land. When men are crooked with God they lose respect for one another. Without Christ, a man cannot find 'righteousness, peace, or joy,' the characteristics of God's Kingdom. Man must be 'born from above'. A great religious leader of the Jews learned this truth from the lips of Christ. 'Verily, verily, I say unto thee, Except a man be born again, he cannot see the kingdom of God. . . . That which is born of the flesh is flesh; and that which is born of the Spirit is spirit. Marvel not that I said unto thee, Ye must be born again' " (John 3:3,6,7).

I continued, "Man can be religious outwardly without a change of heart. Mere religious formalism does not lead to a vital experience of godliness. A determined renunciation of one's greediness, deceitfulness, and sinfulness, and a positive surrender to the claims of Christ and His demands, leads to the goodness which God desires of every man if the world which He intended is to become a reality. Man must be "born from above" with the Spirit of God in order to become a godly man in a godless world. And for those of us who claim to be God's men, we must keep our hearts with all diligence through biblical thinking, that through the study of God's Word, and led by His Spirit, we may fulfill our calling as the representatives of Christ."

Hindrances to Biblical Thinking

There is no doubt of the fact that godless men cannot live godly lives. Furthermore, they have no interest in thinking biblically. The Bible is the enemy of the godless man, for it rebukes his conduct at every turn. This is bad enough, but there is something which is even worse. Many of us, indeed, too many of us who name the Name of Christ, are just as bad as the godless man, except we have endeavored to find Scriptures to veneer our vices with rationalized virtues which, by the way, do not deceive God. God is not interested in our lip service, only in our life service. In the first chapter of his first epistle, John makes this abundantly clear. "If we say that we have fellowship with him, and walk in darkness, we lie. . . . If we say that we have no sin we deceive ourselves. . . . If we say that we have not sinned, we make him a liar. . . ." (1 John 1:6,8,10). As saints, we seem to be off duty more than we are on duty, living for our Lord. Our arrogance, pride, tempers, deceitfulness, selfishness, and secret sins betray us. Many of us do not study God's Word because it rebukes us. We can rationalize and justify our conduct, but God is not interested in excuses. He is only interested in one thing—confession; not with the lips, but with the heart. He would have us takes sides against ourselves in favor of Him (*see* 1 John 1:9).

When our hearts are wrong because of the evil within, it is bound to show in our conduct. We can be verbally orthodox and at the same time be vitally liberal. God is far more interested in what we are *doing* than what we are *saying*. What we say is governed by our heart, for our mouth is the billboard of our heart (*see* Matthew 15:18).

There are times when Christians use the Scriptures, or rather, misuse them, to avoid doing God's will. A friend of mine fell in love with a girl and came to my home to tell me all about it. When he told me whom she was, I admired his choice. Alice was a beautiful girl who would offset his ruggedness; Alice had money, which was not to be ignored. She had brains to go with her beauty, which would be helpful to my friend; she had great ability, which would prove to be an asset to my friend. Among other things she was a Baptist, as was my friend Bill. But I had reason to believe that she was not a Christian.

Bubbling over with joy and love for his discovery, Bill asked me if I would pray that he might find favor in Alice's sight. I promptly refused by telling him we knew God's mind without praying. Believers and unbelievers are not to be unequally yoked together (*see* 2 Corinthians 6:14). How can two walk together unless they are agreed? (*see* Amos 3:3). I insisted that prayer would be the worst form of spiritual politics, for we would be asking that our will be done instead of God's will. He remonstrated with me, pointing out what a wonderful asset she would be for the Lord if we were to pray that she would come to know Him. I agreed, a witness for the Lord she could be, but not a wife for my friend. When we rationalize our way to doing our own will as opposed to the will of God, we are headed for trouble. When we begin to think biblically, the first truth we discover is that we must always be on the level with God. The psalmist has said: "Commit thy way unto the LORD; trust also in him; and he shall bring it to pass. And he shall bring forth thy righteousness as the light, and thy judgment as the noonday" (Psalms 37:5,6), and Solomon adds: "Trust in the LORD with all thine heart; and lean not unto thine own understanding. In all thy ways acknowledge him, and he shall direct thy paths" (Proverbs 3:5,6). We must determine to be on the level with God if biblical thinking is to be of value to us. Our prayer must be: "Search me, O God, and know my heart: try me, and know my thoughts: And see if there be any wicked way in me, and lead me in the way everlasting" (Psalms 139:23,24).

The Means to Biblical Thinking

"Take my yoke upon you and learn of me," the Saviour said. This indicates that biblical thinking has two outstanding characteristics—knowledge and obedience—knowledge of God's Word, and the obedience of a surrendered will. In His farewell address to His disciples prior to His going to the cross, the Lord Jesus told His disciples that He would send the Holy Spirit, who would bring to their remembrance what He had taught them. Furthermore, the Holy Spirit would continue His ministry in the hearts of believers by causing God's Word to come alive in their hearts. Thus, through the study of the Word and a surrendered will ready to obey the Word, a Christian would come into the full blessing of biblical thinking. The Holy Spirit, as the spirit of truth, uses the Scriptures to teach all men and women what is pleasing to God as far as their lives are concerned. Thus Paul refers to the Scriptures as "the sword of the Spirit" (*see* Ephesians 6:17), and encourages the believer to make the Word a part of his Christian armor. The apostle Peter joins the apostle Paul by exhorting us to feed upon God's Word, that we may grow thereby (*see* 1 Peter 2:2,3). Through the study of God's Word we not only learn how to live a Christ-like life, we also come to know the reason for living such a life. "But sanctify the Lord God in your hearts: and be ready always to give an answer to every man that asketh you a reason of the hope that is in you with meekness and fear" (1 Peter 3:15). Thus we can give an intelligent answer to those who ask us the reason for our Christian conduct.

It may be that some of you who read these pages have no interest in the Bible at all. In fact, you may be aggressively and belligerently opposed to it. Do not be surprised, for the Bible states this is the natural reaction of a person who does not believe in the God of the Bible and has no use for His Word (*see* Romans 8:7,8). Though this may not be true of you, Paul indicates that the man who knows not God is a man who is a victim of mental vanity, heartless cruelty, and deadly self-love (*see* Ephesians 4:17–19). And in his brash pride, he is a man who thinks God and His Word is beneath him—for morons only, as the Greek word for *foolishness* would indicate (*see* 1 Corinthians 2:14). Such a person is continually at war with God.

To you who may be reading this book by chance—or in the Providence of God—continue to read it and give it your unbiased attention. God does not ask you to believe His Word because He is God. He bids you to experiment with it, fulfilling the conditions as you would when working an experiment in the field of chemistry. This was the appeal which our Lord made to those who were opposed to Him in His day. "If any man will do his [God's] will, he shall know of the doctrine, whether it be of God, or whether I speak of myself" (John 7:17). God's Word is sufficient to convince the intellect and to convert the soul if one gives it unprejudiced consideration.

To those of us who would serve our Lord, let us study His Word that we may think His thoughts after Him. When we realize that we have the high privilege to live for Him who died for us, as "new men in Christ Jesus" let us so master the art of biblical thinking that in turn the Bible may master us. Then we shall fulfill the desire of our heavenly Father who would have us ". . . to be conformed to the image of his Son . . ." (Romans 8:29).

3

The Power of Positive Thinking

THE WAY WE THINK often indicates what we are. Thus, the way we think may determine our success or failure in life. God's great gift to man is the power of thought. One of the ways in which we can use it is to think positively. Positive thinking is a popular theme in our day. However, it is based on the shaky foundation of foolish arrogance, wishful thinking, and hopeless fear. It reminds one of the man who boasted of his prowess with a gun. His friend watched him as he endeavored unsuccessfully to bring down birds in their flight. Finally he said, "Look! A miracle: dead birds flying." This man's positive thinking was built on foolish pride.

In a more serious vein, some time ago I heard a speaker explaining the basis for positive thinking. His illustration was very interesting indeed. "Suppose," he said, "you have a wife who hasn't been able to make good morning coffee. For days she has brought you suntanned water which she has mistaken for the brew. Don't be discouraged. Tomorrow is another day. Think positively. She may bring real coffee to you." At the time of my story my wife and I had been married for ten years. Let us suppose she had brought me suntanned water for three thousand six hundred and fifty some-odd days. It would take a powerful lot of positive thinking for me to come to the conclusion that she would be able to make it in the future. This type of positive thinking is nothing more than wishful thinking without any basis whatsoever. I am sure that positive thinking as taught in the Bible would have had the man get up after the first week and make the coffee for his wife and serve it to her.

The positive thinking of the apostle Paul was not based on foolish pride, wishful thinking, or hopeless fear, but upon the living reality of Jesus Christ, whom he found not wanting in all of his trials and troubles. Well might the apostle have sung, had it been written:

My hope is built on nothing less
Than Jesus' blood and righteousness;
I dare not trust the sweetest frame,
But wholly lean on Jesus' name.

His oath, His covenant, His blood
Support me in the whelming flood;
When all around my soul gives way,
He then is all my hope and stay.

On Christ, the solid Rock, I stand—
All other ground is sinking sand. . . .

EDWARD MOTE

A study of Paul's letters sets before us three great principles which form the basis of his positive thinking. First of all, he had no mental reservation as to the power of the Gospel. "So, as much as in me is, I am ready to preach the gospel to you that are at Rome also. For I am not ashamed of the gospel of Christ: for it is the power of God unto salvation to every one that believeth; to the Jew first, and also to the Greek" (Romans 1:15,16).

The apostle Paul wholly trusted the Lord Jesus Christ as his Saviour. "Whereunto I am appointed a preacher, and an apostle, and a teacher of the Gentiles. For the which cause I also suffer these things: nevertheless I am not ashamed: for I know whom I have believed, and am persuaded that he is able to keep that which I have committed unto him against that day" (2 Timothy 1:11,12).

Finally, the apostle Paul realized that in Christ he would have the strength and everything it would take to meet the most wretched circumstances of life. "I can do all things through Christ which strengtheneth me. . . . But my God shall supply all your need according to his riches in glory by Christ Jesus" (Philippians 4:13,19). Thus, he is able to write to the believers in Rome that they can be more than conquerors through Him who loved them, even Jesus Christ our Lord (*see* Romans 8:37).

In the first chapter of his letter to the Philippians, the apostle Paul gives us a record of his positive thinking in negative situations. He discusses positive thinking in the light of a personal limitation (1:12–14); then he discusses the possibility of positive thinking in the light of social tension (1:15–19); finally, he gives the secret of positive thinking in the hour of approaching death (1:20–24).

Personal Limitations

Paul had been a great missionary in times past. He had traveled throughout the known world of that day in order to spread the good news of the Gospel, to bring people to the saving knowledge of the Lord Jesus Christ, and to strengthen the believers in their most holy faith. Now he is at the end of his ministry, under the protective custody of Rome, dwelling in Caesar's house. For an active man, this could have been very frustrating. He is concerned about the brethren who have supported him through the years. Thus he writes:

But I would ye should understand, brethren, that the things which happened unto me have fallen out rather unto the furtherance of the gospel; So that my bonds in Christ are manifest in all the palace and in all other places; And many of the brethren in the Lord, waxing confident by my bonds, are much more bold to speak the word without fear.

Philippians, 1:12–14

A careful study of Paul's ministry, as found in the book of the Acts, shows the many distressing and wretched experiences in his ministry for Christ. He gives a good summary of it when writing to the Corinthians.

> Of the Jews five times did I receive forty stripes save one. Thrice was I beaten with rods, once I was stoned, thrice I suffered shipwreck, a night and a day I have been in the deep; In journeyings often, in perils of waters, in perils of robbers, in perils by my own countrymen, in perils by the heathen, in perils in the city, in perils in the wilderness, in perils in the sea, in perils among false brethren; In weariness and painfulness, in watching often, in hunger and thirst, in fastings often, in cold and nakedness. Beside those things that are without, that which cometh upon me daily, the care of all the churches.
>
> 2 Corinthians 11:24–28

If the apostle Paul had been like us, whining and complaining about every little thing, doubtless he would have written the following letter to the church at Philippi:

Dear Brethren:

I want you to know that I am in trouble. I am in protective custody and I feel that the Lord has abandoned me. I want you to know that I do not like it, I resent it, and as far as serving the Lord further, I have decided to forget it.

Who has been more faithful than I in the service of the Lord? Who has traveled more miles and gone to such trouble to be sure that the Gospel would be declared throughout the world? Who has established more churches and brought more people to the saving knowledge of the Lord Jesus Christ? What have I gotten out of it? Nothing but trouble, wretchedness, and distress.

And now I find myself under the protective custody of Rome. I am not permitted to leave the city. I am frustrated, and I want you to know that I do not like it. Furthermore, since I do not intend to serve the Lord further, you may as well give the support which you are accustomed to send to me to someone else.

Yours in Him,
Paul

I quickly add that Paul did not write such a letter. Let me tell you what he might have written:

Dear Brethren:

I wish you were here. I thought I was at the end of my ministry, but I have only reached a new beginning. Do you know that in all of my missionary labors this is the first time that I haven't had to go on deputation to raise funds? The Roman government has decided to pay all the expenses. Furthermore, I do not need to be bothered with traveling, because the government is bringing the congregation to me. In fact, they have been so considerate that they have given me a captive audience. They think I am the prisoner. If they only knew! They fasten the people—guards—to me, which gives me the opportunity to deal with them personally.

True, they think I am very irrational, and they can't wait to tell their fellows how crazy I am. When they are questioned they tell their fellow guards what I have told them, they do not realize they are my missionaries.

So, dear Philippians, don't be discouraged because of my imprisonment. I have discovered a new mission field, and you will be glad to hear that souls are being saved. And since the Roman government is looking after me, the support you generally send to me send to another faithful missionary who is in greater need. Do not worry about me, just rejoice for this marvelous opportunity which is given to me to preach the Gospel, even from Caesar's household.

Yours in Him,
Paul

You may wonder what my imagination is based upon. Turn to the last chapter of the Philippian Epistle. In sending his greetings, Paul is joined by the saints of Rome, and ". . . chiefly they that are of Caesar's household" (Philippians 4:22). These latter had come to know the Lord through Paul's prison ministry. Though Paul tells us of his many trials, at the same time we see that the joy of the Lord was his strength. He writes: "We are troubled on every side, yet not distressed; we are perplexed, but not in despair; Persecuted, but not forsaken; cast down, but not destroyed; Always bearing about in the body the dying of the Lord Jesus, that the life also of Jesus might be made manifest in our body" (2 Corinthians 4:8–10). And Paul might well have added in the "slanguage" of our day "down, but not out."

What was the secret of Paul's victorious spirit? The answer is to be found in verse thirteen of our study. "So that my bonds in Christ are manifest in all the palace and in all other places" (Philippians 1:13). Instead of showing his Roman chains, he demonstrated his bonds in Christ under the most trying circumstances. Paul did not believe in the silly doctrine of our day which maintains that you can accept Christ as Saviour but not as Lord. From the very moment of his conversion Christ was his Lord. And if Christ was his Lord, he had to be Christ's slave. In the opening chapter in the Epistle to the Romans he makes this definitely clear, "Paul, a servant of Jesus Christ, called to be an apostle, separated unto the gospel of God" (1:1). He served the Gospel of God's Son with everything he had (1:9). And when he set out to preach, he had no mental reservations concerning his message (1:15,16). Paul was not ashamed of the Gospel of Christ.

Is it possible for us today to be as victorious as was the apostle Paul? Some time ago, I visited a home for the aged. After dinner, the matron asked me to visit a little old lady who was a victim of arthritis, bent double and in constant pain. She was unable to come down to the dining room to be with the other guests. Her room was her prison. As we ascended the steps, I thought that I would hear all about her troubles. I wondered what I would have to say to her. After we were introduced, she took me by the hand and began to tell me about the sufficiency of God's grace, the wonder of His love, and the richness of His mercy. Not one word about her arthritis, not one complaint about her imprisonment in her room, not one groan concerning her physical agony. Even I could see through the lattice lines of pain the glory of God in her face. What was this woman doing? She was doing in her Boston "prison" what Paul was doing in his Roman prison—showing forth the bonds of Christ. And I have no doubt that she was an encouragement to those round about her as Paul was to those round about him.

Social Contention

Paul not only suffered a limitation of movement, he also suffered at the hands of his fellow believers as well. It is bad enough to be deviled by the world, but it is disgusting indeed when one of Christ's own would destroy you unjustly. Hear his testimony!

And many of the brethren in the Lord, waxing confident by my bonds, are much more bold to speak the word without fear. Some indeed preach Christ even of envy and strife; and some also of good will: the one preach Christ of contention, not sincerely, supposing to add affliction to my bonds: But the other of love, knowing that I am set for the defense of the gospel.

Philippians 1:14–17

It is interesting to note that these hateful brethren who would destroy the apostle were "brethren." They were not nominal Christians. They were not Liberals. They were genuine "brethren in the Lord." They thought they were doing the Lord a favor by destroying Paul. Their hatred was calculated (1:16). They planned Paul's destruction. They hoped to make him more trouble than did the Roman government. And if Paul had our current evangelical spirit, he would have thrown up his hands, left the church, and would have called it quits! But Paul was not a modern evangelical. His faith was not imaginary. His faith was real! Consequently, he was more than conqueror through his loving Saviour, even in this wretched situation.

How could he be victorious? He gives us the answer. He majored not in the believers who were against him but in the believers who were for him, for keep in mind, there were two groups of believers. While he was being persecuted by the one, he rejoiced in the other. These were "of good will." They loved the apostle, and they knew he was set for the defense of the Gospel (*see* Philippians 1:15,17). When we are in a similar situation, the reason we are defeated rather than victorious is because we major on the people who are annoying us and are not relying upon the people supporting us. Paul makes this very clear, for he writes: "What then? Notwithstanding, every way, whether in pretense, or in truth, Christ is preached; and I therein do rejoice, yea, and I will rejoice. For I know that this shall turn to my salvation [my deliverance] through your prayer and the supply of the Spirit of Jesus Christ" (Philippians 1:18,19).

I am not quite sure that I have reached this state of grace, as did the apostle Paul when he was able to say: "Even though they are devilling me, and using Christ as a poison arrow to shoot me down, at least the Gospel is going forth." It is wonderful that there are far more people who are *for* us than there are those who are *against* us. And it would be good for us to keep this in mind. All of us have as much of the Holy Spirit as we need to be the victor of our circumstances instead of their victim.

Approaching Death

Our apostle was not only interested in glorifying the Lord in life, but in death as well.

> According to my earnest expectation and my hope, that in nothing I shall be ashamed, but that with all boldness, as always, so now Christ shall be magnified in my body, whether it be by life, or by death. For to me to live is Christ, and to die is gain. But if I live in the flesh, this is the fruit of my labour: yet what I shall choose I wot not. For I am in a strait betwixt two, having a desire to depart, and to be with Christ; which is far better: Nevertheless, to abide in the flesh is more needful for you.
>
> Philippians 1:20–24

Are you afraid to die? There can be no doubt of the fact that the greatest enemy of man is death. Men everywhere, especially those who have no hope in Christ, are afraid of death.

Some time ago, when flying to the West Coast, I talked to the doctor who was my seat companion. He was to speak to a medical association on various diseases. He discussed with me some of these diseases upon which he would address the meeting. Then he wanted to know why I was going to the Coast. I told him that a friend of mine had died and that I was going to conduct the funeral service. This brought up the question of the matter of death and ways of dying. He then asked me, "How would you like to die?" I responded that I was a coward and that I wanted to die in my sleep. He asked me for my second choice. I told him I preferred to die in a plane crash because it was fast, complete, and profitable from the point of view of insurance. The stewardess who was standing by was shocked. Upon recovery, she asked, "Aren't you afraid to die?"

I replied, "From one point of view, I am, since anything that is new is rather 'iffy'. And since I never died before, the thought of death is somewhat terrifying. However, from another point of view, I am not afraid to die. As a Christian, I believe that if the plane were to go down with my body, my spirit would ascend to be in the presence of my Lord.''

She said, "What's the matter?"

"Nothing," I replied.

"I'm not talking to you," she continued, "your friend is getting white."

The doctor had turned white at the very thought of dying. I pointed out to her that it was not the crash of the plane that was really frightening, but one's destination after the crash. I explained to her how the Bible tells us that in a crash we can land in heaven or hell, granted that our bodies—the house in which we live—would go down with the plane. To know Christ as Saviour would head us for heaven, to reject Him as Saviour would head us for hell.

Paul knew his destination well. "For me to live is Christ, and to die is gain" (Philippians 1:21). Death was not the end of life for the apostle. He did not plan to be buried in a cold, cold, grave. Nor did he plan to have a funeral service where his friends and relatives would come to view his remains while passing a complimentary insult, "My, doesn't he look natural!" Paul knew that death was nothing more than crossing the line from time into eternity, from being a pilgrim on earth to being at home in heaven, and to see our Lord by sight whom we have taken by faith through the years (see 2 Corinthians 5:6–8). Thus Paul describes death as the final journey, ". . . to depart and to be with Christ; which is far better" (Philippians 1:23).

Some of you who read these pages know that you do fear death. Even your fear is an evidence of God's grace, for it is His way to have you prepare yourself to meet it. The reason you fear death is because you have made no preparation for it. Furthermore, you know instinctively that some day you must meet God. This is a date with destiny you cannot avoid (Hebrews 9:27), Recently, in one of our slick magazines, there was a cartoon which depicted a clergyman with his trustees in a business meeting. By their look of sophistication one could tell that they were the kind of men who would tell their secretaries to tell those who phoned that they were out. The cartoon showed the secretary coming into the room with a message for the clergyman. Looking at him, with her right hand and pointed finger upward toward heaven, she gasped, "He's on line three!" When God calls, man *will* answer. "And as it is appointed unto men once to die, but after this the judgment." And in that fateful hour, God will ask every man, "What right have you to come into *my* heaven?" Apart from Christ, man has no right to enter heaven; but with Christ, man can answer God, "The One at your right hand, my interceding Saviour, gives *me* the right to enter *your* heaven."

To those of you who know the Lord Jesus Christ as your Saviour, are you afraid to die? Oh, of course we shall have some fear, for the novel experience is always frightening. But we do not need to be terrified, for though we do not know the nature of eternity, one thing we can know is that God is going to be kind to us (see Ephesians 2:7). And if God is going to be kind to us through the ages, how can we be frightened? One of the things that Jesus accomplished on the cross was the right to deliver us from the fear of death.

The writer to the Hebrews makes this very clear:

> Forasmuch then as the children are partakers of flesh and blood, he also himself likewise took part of the same; that through death he might destroy him that had the power of death, that is the devil; And to deliver them who through fear of death were all their lifetime subject to bondage.
>
> Hebrews 2:14,15

Death for the believer is not to appear before the Judge of the universe; death for us is to go home to our heavenly Father and our

Lord. Christ took the judgment which we deserved upon Him at Calvary (*see* John 5:24). The only thing before us in the coming ages is the kindness of God through the manifestation of His exceeding grace to us.

Some time ago, the wife of a friend of mine died, and he was left with four little children. He tried to explain to the children what had happened to their mother. He had no success until the day of the funeral. To a child, death can be a traumatic experience. As they were on their way to the funeral service, their car was stopped at a traffic light. In front of them was a huge trailer truck casting its shadow upon the side of a hill. At once my friend had the illustration which would make death meaningful to the children. To his young daughter he said, "Laurie, which would you prefer: to be run over with a truck or to be run over with its shadow?" Quickly the little one answered, "Daddy! Don't be silly! A shadow can't hurt you!" "That's right," said the father, "nineteen hundred years ago the blessed Lord Jesus was run over with the truck; yesterday Mother was only run over with the shadow."

"Yea, though I walk through the valley of the shadow of death, I will fear no evil: for thou art with me . . ." (Psalms 23:4). Death may be dark for the one without Christ, but who can be in death's darkness when in the presence of the Light of the world. Not the truck! The shadow only! And well may we continue with the psalmist:

. . . thy rod and thy staff they comfort me. Thou preparest a table before me in the presence of mine enemies; thou anointest my head with oil; my cup runneth over. Surely goodness and mercy shall follow me all the days of my life: and I will dwell in the house of the LORD forever.

Psalms 23:4–6

Thus we have seen that Paul's positive thinking is not wishful thinking. It is not based on arrogant pride, nor is it haunted with hopeless fear. His positive thinking was based upon the death of Christ and His resurrection. Since the apostle's positive thinking was based upon the reality of Christ's work of salvation, he could have the stamina to meet a personal limitation, sufficient grace to love those who would destroy him, and courage to meet approaching death, because for him it was going home. We can do the same in Christ, our risen Lord. For we can sing:

> When he shall come with trumpet sound,
> O may I then in him be found;
> Dressed in his righteousness alone,
> Faultless to stand before the throne.
>
> On Christ, the solid Rock, I stand—
> All other ground is sinking sand. . . .

EDWARD MOTE

4

The Power of Negative Thinking

THOUGH WE MAY not be accustomed to positive thinking, we certainly are masters at negative thinking. How many of us have the courage to think the best of a situation if the worst is possible? If I have mislaid my wallet, my first thought is that someone has taken it. If my wife says that she will be home at a certain hour and she isn't, the first thing that comes to my mind is: *Did she have an accident?* I forget that, being a woman, I should never have taken her at her word insofar as the time of her arrival was concerned.

Humility is a very deceitful way in which to think negatively. You ask a person to sing or play and he replies that he is not able to sing, or in the other case, play. Being brash, I say to them, "Don't tell me you can't play! I know your ability! You insult my intelligence. If you do not want to play, say so! But don't deceive me with your humility."

There are times, however, when people are forced to think negatively because of some disastrous experience which they have had. They have tried their best to please someone, only to receive scornful criticism in return. Thus, they have lost confidence in themselves. Sometimes, in a home, parents may put their children at a disadvantage when comparing a bright child with another who may not have the same ability as the other. Again, a father who is a perfectionist puts his children down simply because they do not meet his rigid standards. In this highly competitive world, we can't all be winners. Consequently, since we can't all reach the top, we become victims of negative thinking.

Moses was known for many things; he was a great leader, a law-giver, and above all, a great servant of God. He accomplished many things, but in the process he lost a great privilege because of his negative thinking. He was forbidden to go into the Promised Land with his people. Israel, as we shall see, gave him many reasons to think negatively, for they were nothing but trouble to him. However, he in turn was a trouble to God by continually refusing God's commission to lead the people out of Egypt, through the wilderness, and into the Land of Promise. Moses ran out of excuses and God ran out of patience. Thus, Moses lost a privilege because he would not take the responsibility of leadership.

In our study of the life of Moses, there are three things we shall want to consider: the occasion for his negative thinking, the reason for his negative thinking, and the tragic result of his negative thinking.

The Occasion

Moses is returning to Egypt from an extended visit with his father-in-law, who lives in Midian. Nearing home, he beholds a wonderful sight. A bush is burning. It is not burning up or down, it is just burning. Fascinated by what he sees, Moses stops to examine this strange event more closely. Suddenly he hears the voice of God speaking to him. Moses is told to take off his shoes, for he is standing on holy ground. God tells Moses He has heard the cry of His people because of their suffering at the hands of their taskmasters. Israel is to be delivered from their bondage. Then Moses receives his commission, "Come now therefore, and I will send thee unto Pharaoh, that thou mayest bring forth my people the children of Israel out of Egypt" (Exodus 3:10).

Moses is amazed at the sight, astonished at God's command, and fearful of the undertaking. The reason he left Egypt was because of some trouble the Hebrews had given him. He had seen an Egyptian and a Hebrew quarreling with one another. Taking the side of the

Hebrew, Moses slew the Egyptian. On another day, he saw two Hebrews fighting and tried to mediate the matter; one of the pair accused Moses of having slain the Egyptian. Moses knew that he could not stay in Egypt because Pharaoh would have him killed when he heard of it (*see* Exodus 2:11–15). Thus he fled to Midian to the home of Jethro, his father-in-law. And now God would have him lead the children of Israel—this troublesome people—out of Egypt. What an occasion for negative thinking; how could he refuse?

In attempting to refuse the Lord, it is not only necessary to have a good excuse, it must be "spiritual" as well. Moses does this very artfully. "And Moses said unto God, Who am I, that I should go unto Pharaoh, and that I should bring forth the children of Israel out of Egypt?" (Exodus 3:11). At once it can be seen that Moses feigns humility, not because he is spiritual, but because he is deceitful. He knows the trouble that Israel will be if he is to lead them from Egypt.

Unfortunately for Moses, God knew the life of Moses from his very birth. He had been found in a little basket by the bank of the river Nile. His sister saw that he was found by Pharaoh's daughter, suggested that a nurse would be a help to her, and had Moses' own mother become the nurse. Moses was brought up in the royal family as one of their own. He became acquainted with the culture, history, politics, and religion of the country. Who was better equipped than he to become Israel's leader (*see* Exodus 2:1–10)? And yet he says to God, "Who am I to lead the people out of Egypt?"

God takes this occasion to reassure Moses that He will be with him by revealing to him His covenant Name by which Israel will know God hereafter. Not only will He be known as the God of their fathers—Abraham, Isaac, and Jacob: He will now be known as the God of the Covenant—Jehovah—the God who was, the God who is, and the God who will be. The God who will become many things to Israel (*see* Exodus 3:12–15). Furthermore, God informs Moses that though the task will be difficult, and Pharaoh will do everything he can to keep Israel in Egypt, He will take this opportunity to show His mighty miracles and wonders in Egypt that will force Pharaoh to let the people go (*see* Exodus 3:16–22).

Moses still doesn't want to carry out God's command. Since the first excuse failed, Moses will try something else. He turns to the unbelief of Israel. "And Moses answered and said, But, behold, they will not believe me, nor hearken unto my voice: for they will say, the LORD hath not appeared unto thee" (Exodus 4:1).

God pleads patiently with Moses. He gives him a miraculous rod which will become the sign of Moses' authority. Then the Lord gives him the power to do two miracles which becomes for Moses the sign of divine authority. God provides him with a third miracle, just in case the other two are not sufficient to convince Israel that he is from God (*see* Exodus 4:2–9).

By this time, Moses is quite frustrated. How can he get ahead of God? At last, he thinks of his limitation—stuttering. This should enable God to see that he, as a leader, would be handicapped to speak to the people and Pharaoh. Moses knows that he cannot refuse God outright. He must be "spiritual" even though he is rebellious. "And Moses said unto the LORD, O my Lord, I am not eloquent, neither heretofore, nor since thou has spoken unto thy servant: but I am slow of speech, and of a slow tongue" (Exodus 4:10). Notice Moses' "spiritual" approach in the expression "O my Lord. . . ." It is true that leadership demands the ability to speak, and when one stutters it can be a real problem, especially if you have to stutter in Hebrew. Thus, we cannot blame Moses for trying this excuse in refusing to accept God's will. There is something dangerous in Moses' excuse. He accuses God of being indifferent to his stuttering. "I am not eloquent, neither heretofore, *nor since thou hast spoken unto thy servant*" (italics mine). How true it is that when we do not want to please the Lord, and we cannot justify our resistance, we try to find something to blame on Him. Of course, we are very "spiritual" about it. Moses is truly a past master at the art of resisting God.

God continues to plead patiently with Moses by assuring him that he need not fear his limitation. God promises to be with him: "And the LORD said unto him, Who hath made man's mouth? or who maketh the dumb, or deaf, or the seeing, or the blind? have not I the LORD? Now therefore go, and I will be with thy mouth, and teach thee what thou shalt say" (Exodus 4:11,12). In a later chapter we shall discuss the nature of suffering as it relates to surrendered thinking. Suffice it now to say that according to God's sovereign will some of His own have been chosen to suffer affliction, not as a means of chastisement or judgment because of sin, but as a means to become the verifying data of the sufficiency of God's grace, under every conceivable condition. God would be with Moses' mouth to teach him what to say. Moses preferred to worship his limitation rather than to abide in the adequacy of his God.

What happens when an individual runs out of excuses and still resists the opportunity to please God? There is only one thing left—stupidity. Moses clearly shows us how to be stupid in such a situation, "And he said, O my Lord, send, I pray thee, by the hand of him whom thou wilt send" (Exodus 4:13). How many times must Moses be told that God wants him to go and be Israel's leader? Was he not listening to God? Wasn't he paying attention to what God was saying? Obviously not! Why listen if you do not want to do what is being asked of you? Moses was determined to have his own way. Later in this study we shall see how this led to tragedy for Moses. To have our way only leads to sorrow and wretchedness.

God has had it. No longer is He patient with Moses. His soul is sizzling (Hebrew text) with anger.

And the anger of the LORD was kindled against Moses, and he said, Is not Aaron the Levite thy brother? I know that he can speak well. And also, behold, he cometh forth to meet thee: and when he seeth thee, he will be glad in his heart. And thou shalt speak unto him, and put words in his mouth: and I

will be with thy mouth, and with his mouth, and will teach
you what ye shall do.''

Exodus 4:14,15

Then the Lord bids Moses return to Egypt and not to worry about
the trouble he had before, because the men were dead and times
had changed (*see* Exodus 4:17–22).

The Reason

Moses certainly had many occasions to be negative. But what
was the reason for it? We know that he had trouble with Israel.
Could there be a deeper reason? The reason for his negative spirit is
quite clear. When we seek to do our own will invariably we are
going to see everything that happens to us in the light of our experience and our fear, and not in the light of opportunities and privi-
leges which surround us to help us in difficult times. This was
Moses' problem. He was so full of himself that he did not listen to
God. God offered to help him, but he refused the divine aid. He
saw Israel as a burden; he saw Pharaoh as a king to be feared. He
totally ignored God's promise to be with him, and how in a miraculous way, He would deliver Israel and Moses from Egyptian bondage. All one needs to do is to examine the complaints that Moses
addresses to God to find this to be true.

Moses and Aaron go to Pharaoh and ask that Israel may go and
worship their God. The King scornfully refuses to let them go.
''Who is this God of the Hebrews?'' he would know. ''What does
He mean to me?'' The request only provokes the monarch to in-
crease the work of the Hebrews and deprive them of the straw to
make bricks. Now they must get it for themselves. Furthermore,
the taskmasters become more harsh, and their cruelty increases.
God had told Moses this would happen, but Moses either ignored it
or forgot it (*see* Exodus 3:18–20; 5:1–9).

The officers of the Hebrews, hearing the cries of the people, go to Aaron and Moses and beg for relief. In turn, Moses comes to God and accuses Him of having no interest in the people since He has brought them no relief. "And Moses returned unto the LORD, and said, Lord, wherefore hast thou so evilly entreated this people? why is it that thou hast sent me? For since I came to Pharaoh to speak in thy name, he hath done evil to this people; neither hast thou delivered thy people at all" (Exodus 5:22,23). When we walk in our own light, we can never walk in the light of God. Selfwill is always destructive. Moses knew the agony of it.

However, God is still patient with His prophet. Again He reassures him that He will be with him. God reminds Moses of the Covenant He has made with him and his people. God has not forgotten Israel's suffering at the hands of the Egyptians. God would have Moses assure the people that He will care for them as He has promised (*see* Exodus 6:1–9). The people will not listen to Moses. They are in open rebellion. Then Moses and Aaron go to Pharaoh only to be rebuffed. In deep discouragement, Moses again returns to the Lord only to complain and accuse God of faithlessness (*see* Exodus 6:30).

Space does not permit us to follow the trials of Moses in Egypt. God shows His mighty works, and finally Israel leaves Egypt. God's great sign of deliverance is the Passover night when the first-born male children of the Egyptians were slain. Pharaoh had been warned of the coming judgment, but he refused to heed the warning. Because of this tragic event, Pharaoh is forced to let the people go.

Moses' troubles are not at an end. The people complain because they are forced to leave Egypt. They accuse Moses of bringing them to the wilderness to die (*see* Exodus 14:10–12). God supplies them with manna in the wilderness, but they complain about it. Then they think they will die of thirst. Apart from his own selfwill, Moses really finds Israel a burden to him.

Moses now faces the tragedy of his own stubborness. God sum-

mons Moses to Mt. Sinai in order to receive the Ten Commandments. He spends forty days and nights with God. On one of these
days God advises Moses that Israel is corrupt and has gone into
idolatry. Joshua and Moses descend from the Mount to see what is
happening. When they come within sight of the people, Moses
becomes very angry at the idolatrous conduct he beholds.

For while Moses and Joshua are with the God on the Mount, the
people and Aaron are at the foot of the mountain. The people begin
to complain to Aaron. "We do not know where God is, nor can we
find Moses! Make us a god so we can worship him." Aaron takes a
collection from the people, and from it makes a golden calf. "Here
is your god," he cries. The people worship it and engage in other
forms of pagan conduct. It is this scene which Moses and Joshua
witness when they come to the people.

Moses is so angry that he breaks the tablets of stone on which
were written the Commandments. Then he smashes the golden calf,
crushes and burns it, throws the crushed powder upon the water and
makes Israel drink it. He rebukes Aaron for leading the people into
idolatry and demands that the people return to God. (*see* Exodus
32:1–29).

Moses returns to the Lord to plead for Israel. God in His anger
would destroy them. At this point, Moses comes through with flying colors. "And Moses returned unto the LORD and said, Oh, this
people hath sinned a great sin, and have made them gods of gold.
Yet now, if thou wilt forgive their sin—; and if not, blot me, I pray
thee, out of thy book which thou has written" (Exodus 32:31,32). I
have no doubt that Moses was not only angry with Aaron and the
people, he was also angry with himself. He knew that Aaron was
his idea, not God's. Through his self-will Moses brought all this
trouble upon himself. But when the reality dawned upon him he
was willing to take the responsibility for it. "Blot me out of thy
book." He was willing to die for the people that they might be
forgiven. This would have been a tragic price to pay for negative,
stubborn thinking, but God intervened with His grace.

Our tale is almost told, but for a tragic note which should warn us all against the perils of negative thinking.

The Tragedy

In our study thus far we have seen how patient God has been with Moses. One would think that Moses would have learned to be patient with Israel. When anyone takes the place of leadership, it stands to reason that one thing he must be is patient with those whom he is to lead. Granted that the people to be led can try him to the utmost. Israel was a burden to Moses, trying his patience at every turn of the road. The people cry for meat (*see* Numbers 11:1,4). Miriam and Aaron are jealous of Moses because God speaks directly to him and not to them (*see* Numbers 12:1–16). The people continue to grumble in their rebellion (*see* Numbers 14:1–4). Moses has no peace at all. We can easily understand why he should be impatient with them. God had promised to be with him, but Moses was so near the people and God seemed so far away.

We come to a day when the people cry for water. The land is barren, nothing can be grown, there is no food for their cattle (*see* Numbers 20:1–5). In desperation, Moses and Aaron go before the Lord to plead for water. God bids them to speak to the rock, out of which water will flow, enough for the people and their cattle. Moses gathers the people together before the rock, but he is angry with the people. He doesn't speak to the rock, he yells at the people: ". . . Hear now, ye rebels; must we fetch you water out of this rock? And Moses lifted up his hand, and with his rod he smote the rock twice: and the water came out abundantly, and the congregation drank, and their beasts also." (Numbers 20:10,11). Moses loses his cool. He becomes impatient with the people. God has reason to be impatient with him, but He isn't. Moses has no right to be impatient with the people.

As a result, Moses loses a great privilege. He cannot go into the

Promised Land with the people. Listen to what God tells him, "And the LORD spake unto Moses and Aaron, Because ye believed me not, to sanctify me in the eyes of the children of Israel, therefore ye shall not bring this congregation into the land which I have given them (Numbers 20:12).

Moses was stunned at the Lord's words. Several times, as recorded in the Book of Deuteronomy, Moses pleaded with God to enter the Land, but God told him the question was closed.

The great lesson we can learn from the life of Moses is that negative thinking is dangerous, especially where God is concerned. He will be patient with us to a point, but after that, there is a point of no return. God promised to be with Moses in every circumstance. Moses preferred his own will and way. As a result, he lost one of his greatest desires, to enter the Promised Land with his people. Let us heed the record and think positively with God, so we do not miss a privilege because we haven't taken the responsibility that accompanies it.

5

The Power
of Transformed Thinking

IN THE PREVIOUS CHAPTER, we saw how Moses lost a privilege because of his negative thinking. If there is anything worse than negative thinking, it is that thinking which is born of a bitter spirit. A bitter spirit may be the result of unjust treatment. It also may be the result of a traumatic experience. Again, it may be the result of always being put at a disadvantage by people who should know better. And what may you think of an intimate friend who turns on you and deals with you most treacherously?

Many a man has given faithful service to a company and has worked his way up to a given position which he has desired, only to see it given to another for political reasons. Beverly Sills, the world famous opera singer became bitter to the point where she stopped singing because of two of her children; one was born deaf,· the other mentally retarded. It was through the efforts of the opera company she sang for, which helped her over this tragic period, that we can hear her lovely voice again. Sometimes parents are unthinking in comparing one child to the disadvantage of the other, which causes bitterness in the child who is less favored.

Bitterness is not a rational trait, it is an emotional one. It is born of fear and insecurity, when a crisis hits us. A young man with brilliant prospects in the company for which he works suddenly is blinded in an accident. What will he do? How can he manage? Will his wife continue to love him? How can the poor fellow answer these questions when he has lived in a world of sight? Now he must live in a world of darkness. One can understand why he would be bitter, for he thinks of the future in terms of fear and uncertainty.

The most tragic form of bitter thinking is when a person believes that God has been unfaithful to him. A beloved mother is ill. The family has trustfully looked to God for her healing. They are faithful to Him, they have obeyed His Word. They have tried to please Him daily. But as they pray the mother's condition worsens, and finally she dies. What sorrow! What bitterness! Another heart is broken, and because of the fear of loneliness, bitterness reigns in that home because God has disappointed the godly family. Didn't God care for them? Was He indifferent to their plea?

Jeremiah experienced such bitterness because of God's apparent indifference to him. In his case, he was so angry with God that he called God a liar. Rebellious Israel provoked him to such a state. God called him to preach to them. God told Jeremiah they would be a troublesome people, and they were. They provoked the prophet to such an extent that he could not stand himself, the enemies of God, or even God Himself. Jeremiah was bitter. But we shall learn how the Word of God changed the heart of Jeremiah from bitterness to joy. There are three things we want to learn from our study: What was the nature of Jeremiah's bitterness? How did the Word of God change the spirit of Jeremiah? Can we expect God and His Word to change the hearts of people today so they can know His peace instead of the bitterness which gnaws as a mental cancer in their hearts?

The Bitterness of Jeremiah

In the fifteenth chapter of the prophecy of Jeremiah, the prophet displays his bitterness:

> I sat not in the assembly of the mockers, nor rejoiced; I sat alone because of thy hand: for thou hast filled me with indig-

nation. Why is my pain perpetual, and my wound incurable,
which refuseth to be healed? wilt thou be altogether unto me
as a liar, and as waters that fail?

                                                    Jeremiah 15:17,18

There can be no doubt of the fact that Jeremiah is upset. As one
of the Lord's servants, he must have been greatly disturbed to call
God a liar. The pain of which he speaks must have been intense,
and the wound to which he refers must have been a dreadful sore.
No doubt Jeremiah expected God to deliver him from this affliction, and since He didn't, he so expressed his disappointment.

It would be interesting to know what kind of "liar" Jeremiah
had in mind when he applied the term to God. He tells us in the
text, he compares God to a failing brook. Jeremiah is a man of the
desert. He knows the heat of the day, the glare of the sun, the grit-
tiness of the sand. He also knows the importance of water to slake
one's thirst in a dry, parched land. When one is overcome with
thirst, there is a tendency to be a victim of a mirage; one sees water
that isn't really there. The water is but a product of the imagination. Walking toward what appears to be a rushing brook of cool
water, one sees upon arriving, that there is just enough water to
tease him but not enough to refresh him. The mirage of the brook is
deceitful. In a like manner, Jeremiah thought God was as deceitful
as the brook. To the prophet, God was a God who dangled His
promises before one's eyes but never fulfilled them. This is the bitterness of Jeremiah.

It is interesting to note that Job in his affliction used the same
picture of the brook to describe the false comfort of his friends.

My brethren have dealt deceitfully as a brook, and as the
stream of brooks they pass away; which are blackish by reason
of the ice, and wherein the snow is hid: What time they wax
warm, they vanish: when it is hot, they are consumed out of

their place. The paths of their way are turned aside; they go to nothing, and perish.

Job 6:15–18

I can believe that many among us have felt the same about God and our friends. We have sought God's aid and our friends' comfort, only to have them fail us. They could have helped us, but they did not! They only teased us as the brook, but gave us no water. Both God and man abandoned us when we needed them most.

What was the nature of Jeremiah's wound that upset him so terribly? We might be surprised to learn that his problem was not physical; it was social and spiritual. His painful wound was Israel, to whom God called him to minister. They were a rebellious, wicked people who had turned from God to idolatry. Jeremiah was sent to Judah to preach a message of judgment and repentance. The people hated Jeremiah because they hated God. Jeremiah was to be God's conscience to them and to appeal to them to return to Him and to obey His Law. Jeremiah's commission is stated very clearly.

Then the LORD put forth his hand, and touched my mouth. And the LORD said unto me, Behold, I have put my words in thy mouth. See, I have this day set thee over the nations and over the kingdoms, to root out, and to pull down, and to destroy, and to throw down, to build, and to plant. . . . Thou therefore, gird up thy loins, and arise, and speak unto them all that I command thee: be not dismayed at their faces, lest I confound thee before them. For, behold, I have made thee this day a defensed city, and an iron pillar, and brasen walls against the whole land, against the kings of Judah, against the princes thereof, against the priests thereof, and against the people of the land. And they shall fight against thee, but they shall not prevail against thee; for I am with thee, saith the LORD, to deliver thee.

Jeremiah 1:9,10,17–19

Anyone who has dealt with people knows that they can have enough problems with friendly people. But to be sent to preach to a rebellious people who hate you is something else again. On top of all this, if one is sensitive, as was Jeremiah, one can see why he was bitter and why he thought that God had left him. With Moses, Jeremiah thought of himself and forgot that God had told him that the people would hate him. God would remind him that when preaching a message of judgment one cannot be expected to be received with open arms by those who are being judged.

In speaking of Israel, that is Judah of the Southern Kingdom, the Lord gives to us His own estimation of them:

> For thus saith the LORD, Thy bruise is incurable, and thy wound is grievous. There is none to plead thy cause, that thou mayest be bound up: thou hast no healing medicines. All thy lovers have forgotten thee; they seek thee not; for I have wounded thee with the wound of an enemy, with the chastisement of a cruel one, for the multitude of thine iniquity; because thy sins were increased. Why criest thou because of thine affliction? thy sorrow is incurable for the multitude of thine iniquity: because thy sins were increased, I have done these things unto thee.
>
> Jeremiah 30:12–15

There is one thing at least for which we can commend Jeremiah; he makes the wound and pain of Israel his wound and pain. Although he is a messenger of judgment, he doesn't forget to show sympathy and mercy as well. We might learn this lesson; when we need to rebuke and judge others, let us do it in the spirit of grace and mercy. Though God had forbidden Jeremiah to fellowship with this sinful people, lest His servant be in a compromising position, Jeremiah still thought of Israel as his people (*see* Jeremiah 15:19,20).

There were times in the ministry of Jeremiah that he felt like turning away from preaching, but the fire of God burned within him. He could not refrain from proclaiming God's Word (*see* Jeremiah 20:8,9).

The Joy of Jeremiah

So many times, as Christians, we read the Bible but we really don't believe it. We give mental assent to its truths and will even defend it against its enemies. Even ministers suffer from this occupational hazard. As long as things are going well we can speak with great authority concerning the greatness of God. When we meet with a crisis, our authority and words vanish into thin air. There is nothing so bitter as to know the way out of a circumstance and not take it. And the reason we do not get out of our troubles is that many times it is the first opportunity to call attention to ourselves in a big way. When we have had enough of our wretchedness, something comes along to change our minds and the direction of our living. This happened to Jeremiah.

One day, Jeremiah found God's Word, read it, and actually believed it. From bitter thinking he changed to joyful faith. Hear him tell it: "Thy words were found and I did eat them; and thy word was unto me the joy and rejoicing of mine heart: for I am called by thy name, O LORD God of hosts" (Jeremiah 15:16). Jeremiah found God's words and "ate" them. How do you, reader, read the word of God? Do you merely massage your eyeballs as you read the type? Or do you take in what you read, understand it, and make it yours? This is exactly what Jeremiah did. To "eat" the Word was to meditate upon it and be influenced by it. When he did this something happened to his life. He had the same people to contend with; he had the same Word of God to preach, but now, it was Jeremiah's Word as well as God's. When Jeremiah had called God a liar he had seen his experiences in the light of his weakness and the people's hatred, now he sees these experiences in the light of

God's power and faithfulness. A given point of view can make a real difference as to how we think and feel in a given situation.

What was the passage of Scripture that Jeremiah found that so changed his life? There is no explicit passage mentioned in the text. But we might choose one which seems to be his testimony to the event. We turn to the Lamentations, chapter three, and read the following: "This I recall to my mind, therefore have I hope. It is of the LORD's mercies that we are not consumed, because his compassions fail not. They are new every morning: great is thy faithfulness" (Lamentations 3:21–23). When writing these words, Jeremiah was in the spirit of reflection. He tells us so in the previous verses (*see* 3:18,20). He remembers how angry he was with God. Now he is at peace with Him. The prophet's former conduct in the light of God's mercy has humbled him. No longer is he the victim of himself, his people, or his sensitivity. He now knows himself to be the victim of God's mercy, compassion, and grace. With the psalmist he could say, "My times are in thy hands: deliver me from the hand of mine enemies, and from them that persecute me" (Psalms 31:15). Now Jeremiah bears testimony to his confidence in the Lord; no longer is he insecure.

As he continues his witness, Jeremiah realizes that it is by God's mercy and compassion that this change has been brought about in his life. The word *consumed* is often used for the concept of death, since in the desert decay is rapid as it eats away the body. Thus God's mercy is more than a theory to Jeremiah. No doubt, the prophet thought of his people in terms of spiritual decay, as those who would soon perish from the earth. God's compassion never fails. Jeremiah knew that he was not worthy of it. The very breath that God gave him he used to curse God. Still God loved him. God's servant who had failed his Lord stood amazed at His wondrous grace.

And what could Jeremiah say about God's faithfulness in the light of his own rebellion? He rejoices that God not only cared for him on a yearly basis, or a monthly or weekly basis, but on a daily basis. "His mercies were new every morning." Doubtless he prayed the prayer of the psalmist:

> O God, thou art my God; early will I seek thee: my soul thirsteth for thee, my flesh longeth for thee in a dry and thirsty land, where no water is; To see thy power and thy glory, so as I have seen thee in the sanctuary. Because thy lovingkindness is better than life, my lips shall praise thee.

> Psalms 63:1–3

For God's mercies came in the morning—at daybreak, the beginning of the day. The prophet rejoiced because he knew that even before noon he could be in trouble. And how wonderful it was for him to start the day with God's mercies. Well might he have sung, had it been written:

> Great is Thy faithfulness,
> Oh God, my Father!
> There is no shadow of turning with Thee;
> Thou changest not, Thy compassions they fail not:
> As Thou has been, Thou forever wilt be.

> Pardon for sin and a peace that endureth,
> Thine own dear presence to cheer and to guide,
> Strength for today and bright hope for tomorrow—
> Blessings all mine, with ten thousand besides!

> THOMAS O. CHISHOLM

The Confidence of Jeremiah

What really made the change in the life of Jeremiah? It was coming to grips with the Word of God, fulfilling its conditions, obeying its precepts, and looking forward to God fulfilling His promises. This is what turned Jeremiah's bitterness to joy. Having cursed

God, now he can rejoice that he is called by God's Name. And let us keep in mind that this is not the testimony of an unbeliever, rather it is a testimony of a son of God, even his servant, who allowed the pressures of life—of "Christian" service—to drive him from his Lord. And in God's Providence there came to him that word that brought him back to his Lord and made him a victor over life's pressures.

Well may we ask the question, "Can God's Word do this for us today? Can we really be transformed people if we learn to think biblically?" To answer these questions, we must ask a few more. "Do we have pressures as did Jeremiah? Do we have God's Word as did Jeremiah? Is God interested in us as He was in His prophet?" We do not need to argue about the first question, for who of us are not subject to the pressures of life, even the Christian life? We have God's Word. We preach it, we teach it, we give witness to it, but like Jeremiah, we do not heed it. The question we must ask ourselves is, "Do we really believe it, or merely give mental assent to it?" God Himself, through Jesus Christ our Lord, promised to be ". . . the same, yesterday, and to day, and for ever" (Hebrews 13:8). But in order to have the joy of Jeremiah we must not only be students of the Bible, we must take it seriously too.

Men of the business world might well say, "How can the Scriptures give me security and courage? We live in a rough, tough competitive world which is deceitful and greedy on every hand. What can the Bible do for me? How can I be honest and just when the competition is unfair and dishonest?" Isaiah answers the question: "Fear thou not; for I am with thee: be not dismayed; for I am thy God: I will strengthen thee; yea, I will help thee; yea, I will uphold thee with the right hand of my righteousness" (Isaiah 41:10). God never overlooks the acts of a righteous man who is in active fellowship with Him.

What comfort does God's Word have today for parents whose children have been brought up in the faith and now are far from the

Lord? The psalmist gives us some comfort. "The steps of a good man are ordered by the LORD: and he delighteth in his way. Though he fall, he shall not be utterly cast down: for the LORD upholdeth him with his hand" (Psalms 37:23,24). To be sure, there are many distressed parents who may be plagued with guilt because their children have not turned out well. In their embarrassment, they have closed their hearts to their children because of the disgrace which has been brought upon the family name. Disgrace has been brought to God also, *but He has not closed His heart.* Good men in whom He has been pleased have fallen away from Him. His desire is to restore them, not to ignore them. No matter how low an individual falls, underneath are the everlasting arms. This passage from God's Word, when thoroughly thought through, can even open the hearts of parents that have been closed to their children because of their conduct.

Finally, there are those who have friends and relatives who have prayed that they might come to know the Lord. Here, again, we can trust the words of one who betrayed the Lord and found forgiveness and restoration in Him. "The Lord is not slack concerning his promise, as some men count slackness; but is longsuffering to us-ward, not willing that any should perish, but that all should come to repentance" (2 Peter 3:9). Peter denied the Lord. The Lord prayed for him. He prayed a prayer that was not answered (*see* Luke 22:31,32). Our Lord knew that Peter would have to learn the hard way. Some people still do! Our prayers should not only contain words on behalf of a lost one, we should illustrate our prayers and concern by living the life of Christ before them also.

Thus it is that there can be tremendous power in transformed thinking as we master the art of biblical thinking. That art is to be learned through a daily study of the Bible and submission to its demands as we are led by the Holy Spirit, but before we can do this, we must be sure that we have new life in Christ by taking Him as our Saviour and Lord.

6

The Power of Faithful Thinking

ONE OF THE MOST frequent questions people ask is, "Why do the righteous suffer?" To be ignorant of this question leads to a confusion in thought, a wretchedness of mind, and to some, even a feeling of guilt. This is particularly true when parents give birth to a child who is physically malformed or mentally retarded. Is there really an answer as to why such things as these happen? Doubtless there are many answers, but none of them seem to satisfy the human heart. We know that some things occur which are the result of an accident. A little boy goes out of the yard into the street and sees larger boys hanging on to the tailboard of a truck. Following their example, he takes hold of the tailboard too, only to be thrown into the path of an oncoming car as the truck gathers speed. The child is killed. We know *what* happened. We know *how* it happened. But *why* did it happen?

There is a natural tendency on the part of people to think that tragic things happen because they have been displeasing to God. Some time ago, while holding a Bible conference in the east, the wife of the pastor was told that she had cancer. Returning from the doctor, she was quite distressed; not because she had been told that she had cancer, but because she believed that God was punishing her because her son was living in gross sin. After talking to her for a time I said, "Let us look to the Lord in prayer and let us praise Him that He isn't as mean as you are." Taken aback, she said, "What do you mean?" I replied that God is not out to seek vengeance on those who displease Him. He is a God of mercy and love. His desire is to restore and not to condemn. Not all suffering is the result of sin, though some suffering is brought about by it. Social diseases bring destruction to the body. The use of drugs may cause a mother to give birth to a deformed son. Drinking to excess can do great damage to an individual. Thus, the reason for suffering is no great mystery.

Turning to the Word of God, we discover that there are a number of reasons why people are afflicted in various ways. On one occasion, our Lord healed a man who had been lame for over thirty-eight years. To this one He said, ". . . Behold, thou art made whole: sin no more, lest a worse thing come unto thee" (John 5:14). Obviously this is an example where a man's sin caused his infirmity. The Lord warns him not to get so involved again. On another occasion, while walking with their Lord, the disciples see a blind man and they attribute his blindness to some sin in his life or that of his parents.

> And as Jesus passed by, he saw a man which was blind from his birth. And his disciples asked him, saying, Master, who did sin, this man, or his parents, that he was born blind? Jesus answered, Neither hath this man sinned, nor his parents: but that the works of God should be made manifest in him.
>
> John 9:1–3

Here is a case where personal sin, or that of anyone else, is not responsible for the man's blindness. There is the added thought that some people are afflicted that God may be glorified through the affliction. We may remember when studying the life of Moses that God has explicitly decreed that there should be afflicted people to show the sufficiency of His grace under every and all conditions of life (*see* Exodus 4:11,12).

In our study, we now turn to the Book of Job, for Job was tremendously interested in the answer to the question, "Why do the righteous suffer?'' Affliction comes to him without any reason whatsoever. He is a godly man who lives a life pleasing to God. Suddenly he loses his wealth, family, and health, and he doesn't know why. He is quite distressed and wretched, as we shall see. He argues with God to see why these things happened to him. It is interesting to note that he never doubts God. He rests in God's sovereignty. He only wants to know why these things happen to him.

The Tests of Job

The text of our study makes it abundantly clear that there was no sin in Job's life that would call forth the afflictions that fell upon him. ''There was a man of the land of Uz, whose name was Job; and that man was perfect and upright, and one that feared God, and eschewed evil'' (1:1). As the word ''perfect'' would indicate, Job was not sinless. No man is sinless, but Job was blameless in the sight of God. He feared God and hated evil. He was a wealthy man in cattle, camels, and sheep. He had a very great household. He was known as the wealthiest man in the east. He also was a family man; he had great fellowship with his children and was careful to look after their spiritual welfare (*see* Job 1:1–5).

Beginning at verse six of the first chapter, we are presented with a scene in heaven, where God has assembled the angelic hosts. Among them is Satan. God inquires what the adversary of men has been doing, and he replies that he has been going up and down the earth checking on the saints. ''And the LORD said unto Satan, Hast thou considered my servant Job, that there is none like him in the earth, a perfect and an upright man, one that feareth God, and escheweth evil?'' (1:8) In so many words Satan answers God: ''Why do You think I am a fool? Why should I test Job when You have bribed him to trust You? What haven't You given him? You have made him the wealthiest man in the east. Take away everything You have given him and he will curse You to Your face! The only reason he trusts You is because of what he can get out of

You'' (*see* 1:9–11). God accepts the challenge and allows Satan to take all that Job possesses. Job is not touched, but his family is slain (see 1:12). Here we begin to see one of the great reasons for suffering which only heaven could reveal. Some believers are chosen to suffer because God would demonstrate to the world that people believe in Him not because He has bribed them, not because He has given them everything they have wanted, but because they really love Him and in their suffering God's grace will prove to be sufficient.

Satan leaves the presence of the Lord, and using the agents of nature and the wickedness of men, strips Job of his wealth and family. To say the least, the events which follow are most traumatic (*see* 1:13–19). Though Job is stunned at what has happened, he rises to great heights of faith which becomes as dust in the devil's eye.

> Then Job arose, and rent his mantle, and shaved his head, and fell down upon the ground, and worshipped, And said, Naked came I out of my mother's womb, and naked shall I return thither: the LORD gave, and the LORD hath taken away; blessed be the name of the LORD. In all this Job sinnned not, nor charged God foolishly.
>
> 1:20–22

In these personally shaking events, Job's stabilizing influence is his absolute belief in the sovereignty of God. Thus he maintains his integrity in the experiences which so trouble him.

In the second chapter the scene takes us back to heaven, where we find the angels reassembled before God with Satan in their midst. God again questions Satan as to his work, and again he has been checking up on the saints. God asked him if he has considered Job to which Satan replies ''No!'' Satan adds, ''You have taken his wealth but if one has to choose between wealth and health, they will choose health. Take his health and he will curse You to Your face'' (*see* 2:1–6). God accepts the challenge; Satan can take his health but not his life.

The adversary of men leaves the presence of the Lord and afflicts Job with boils from the top of his head to his toes. Job sits on an ash heap scraping himself because of the running sores (*see* 2:7,8). To read of Job's appearance may be bilious; Job thought it was loathsome. "My flesh is clothed with worms and clods of dust; my skin is broken, and become loathsome. My days are swifter than a weaver's shuttle, and are spent without hope" (Job 7:5,6).

Many commentators have rebuked Mrs. Job because she seemed so godless in her protest to him, "Give up God and die!" However, I am very sympathetic to her. When a loved one is suffering there is nothing more horrible than the time you have to stand helplessly by his side and cannot help him in his agony. Job was indeed a pitiful sight. Mrs. Job was beside herself in agony. She knew he was a godly man and could not understand why God did not come to her husband's aid. With some scorn she says, ". . . Doest thou still maintain thine integrity? Curse God and die!" (2:9). Not from the ashes, but from the throne of grace Job answers her, ". . . Thou speakest as one of the foolish women speaketh. What? Shall we receive good at the hand of God, and shall we not receive evil? In all this Job did not sin with his lips" (2:10). This is more dust in the devil's eye as he sees Job's faith in God subjected to great pressure.

In his reply to his wife, Job sets before us another important principle. Just because we believe in God, it does not follow that we will not be the victims of evil events. Job is very realistic in his theology. He believes himself to be in a world where God's children will suffer all the things which can happen to the godless. He does not expect God to give him a life of prosperity without some adversity. In so many words he says, "We are not trusting God to see what it will profit us; we trust Him because we love Him." This gave the lie to Satan's charge against Job.

Job's friends soon hear of his difficulty, and they come to comfort him. When they see him they are stunned. They mourn for him. They are so overcome with the tragedy that they cannot speak to him for seven days (*see* 2:11–13).

The Comforters of Job

Though Job was considered blameless and upright in the sight of God, this did not make him so spiritual that he forgot to be human. Like any normal individual he detests the thing that happened to him, and he makes his distress very clear.

> Let the day perish wherein I was born, and the night in which it was said, There is a manchild conceived. Let that day be darkness; let not God regard it from above, neither let the light shine upon it. . . . As for that night, let darkness seize upon it; let it not be joined unto the days of the year, let it not come into the number of the months. . . . Why died I not from the womb? Why did I not give up the ghost when I came out of the belly? . . . For now I should have lain still and been quiet, I should have slept: then had I been at rest.
>
> Job 3:3,4,6,11,13

Having limited vision myself, I can appreciate the wretchedness of the afflicted when they are given glib Christian sympathy. Some time ago, I was asked to speak on the subject of "The Blessing of Limited Vision." I said to the one who made the request, "I haven't heard anything so ridiculous! There is no blessing in limited vision; it is a curse, a downright inconvenience. I'll grant that there is blessing from the Lord, but it is still inconvenient. I have experienced times of frustration even as did Job, but with him, I have retreated to the place of God's sovereignty, where only true peace can be found."

The comforters of Job are "comforters" indeed. Their work is to make him as wretched as possible. They speak from self-righteousness, not from sympathy. They are full of rancid holiness. In their legalism, they suffer from misidentification, mistaking themselves for God Himself. Their advice and "comfort" is worse than the affliction that has befallen Job. They appear to go out of their way to tell him how bad he really is, and they even attribute their viewpoint to God. Each of the friends believe Job to be a sinner and tell him as much. You somehow get the feeling that these men went to a Bible college or seminary and flunked out after the first semester of studies. They learned only one thing: adversity is caused by living a sinful life. They learned nothing more, and if so, they forgot it.

Space does not permit us to discuss the Book of Job in its entirety. Between chapters four and thirty-seven there is a continual conversation between Job and his comforters. They go back and forth over the same ground from many angles. Our purpose here will be to summarize the way in which Job's friends try to convince him that he is a sinner before God. Job's responses indicate how wretched they make him.

Eliphaz is the first to speak. He pays Job a compliment in which there is hidden a nasty rebuke. He points out how Job has been a teacher of many, how he has strengthened the weak, how he has enabled the faltering to stand firm, how he has given courage to the fearful. Then comes the thrust of malice.

> But now it is come upon thee, and thou faintest; it toucheth thee, and thou art troubled. Is not this thy fear, thy confidence, thy hope, and the uprightness of thy way? Remember, I pray thee, who ever perished, being innocent? or where were the righteous cut off? Even as I have seen, they that plow iniquity, and sow wickedness, reap the same.
>
> 4:5–8.

Eliphaz chides Job for not taking his own medicine. He can give it to others, but he can't take his own advice and weather his own storm. His comforting word to Job is "Don't complain, sinner, you got what you deserved!"

Bildad takes his turn to comfort Job. "The reason your sons died is because they had it coming to them. They were sinners, and finally God caught up with them!" Countering Job's arguments he says:

> How long wilt thou speak these things? and how long shall the words of thy mouth be like a strong wind? Doth God pervert judgment? or doth the Almighty pervert justice? If thy children hath sinned against him, and he have cast them away for their transgression; If thou wouldest seek unto God betimes, and make thy supplication to the Almighty; If thou wert pure and upright; surely now he would awake for thee, and make the habitation of thy righteousness prosperous.
>
> 8:2–6

Bildad's final word of comfort to Job is stinging. "Sinners deserve to die. Your sons were sinners. Why complain? They got what they deserved!" Truly, we can be sympathetic to poor Job in the light of the "comfort" he is getting from his friends.

Zophar chimes in with a cutting word of comfort by calling Job foolish and arrogant. Job is stupid and is in need of God's true wisdom. Answering Job's protests, Zophar retorts:

> Should not the multitude of words be answered? and should a man full of talk be justified? Should thy lies make men hold their peace? and when thou mockest, shall no man make thee ashamed? For thou hast said, My doctrine is pure, and I am clean in thine eyes. But oh that God would speak, and open his lips against thee; And that he would shew thee the secrets

of wisdom, that they are double to that which is!. Know therefore that God exacteth of thee less than thine iniquity de-
serveth.

11:2–6

Zophar's final word of comfort. "Job, you're a liar. Why not
shut up? Who are you to talk of your purity and cleanness in God's
sight?" It would seem that each of Job's comforters is playing
"Can you top this?" to see which one of them can make Job feel
most wretched.

This ends round one insofar as the comforters are concerned, and
Job has an answer for each of them. However, our purpose is to
take the highlights of Job's answers, for in the main, Job's con-
troversy is with God. There are two more rounds of arguments; his
comforters sounding the same ignorant note, that Job's troubles are
due to his unrighteousness. Job stoutly refuses to accept their ac-
cusation, for he knows that he is blameless in the sight of God.

Why are Job's comforters so caustic? There is a two-fold answer.
The Law does teach that adversity will come to someone who dis-
obeys God. Sickness can be a form of judgment upon the sinner
(*see* Deuteronomy 28:15,35), but there are other reasons for
sickness or affliction which Job's comforters fail to grasp. Thus,
they are playing their theological violin on one string alone. Another possible reason is that if the righteous *do* suffer, and they do,
what is there to prevent them from suffering the same fate as Job?
To fear the loss of security drives one to rationalize God's truth into
error. They do not intend to think of the possibility of losing their
wealth and health, even if it means hiding from reality by resting in
self-deception.

Finally, the conversation between Job and his friends comes to
an impasse. They cannot convince Job that he is wrong; he insists
that he is right. In this silence, Elihu, the fifth member of the
group, now speaks his piece. He has deferred to the other three

comforters because of his youth. He is angry with Job because of his self-righteousness (*see* 32:1–6). Admitting that he is young and does not have the wisdom of his elders, he does maintain that he has the wisdom of God through inspiration. He also feels that he has the humility God requires them to emulate. He declares he must speak, for God's Spirit is upon him. He will speak, not with fawning words, but with words which are faithful and true (*see* 32:7–22).

Before addressing his remarks to Job, Elihu rebukes the other comforters, not only for criticizing Job but because they have no answer to give him. (*see* 32:3). He expected to hear some wisdom come from the lips of the older men, but concludes that they have nothing to offer. "Great men are not always wise: neither do the aged understand judgment" (32:9). Elihu assures Job that he is speaking from his heart and that he is speaking in God's stead, and furthermore, he tells Job with a touch of arrogance, "I am the kind of comforter from God you really wanted" (*see* 33:1–6).

In an indirect way, Elihu reaches the same conclusion as the other three comforters, except he takes a more positive attitude in doing it. First of all, he tells Job that he should stop striving against God, for the mind of the Almighty cannot be changed (*see* 33:13). God endeavors to warn men through dreams to avoid a course of action which will bring them to a tragic end. In these warnings, God does everything to protect man against himself. If a man is truly righteous, God will protect him from harm (*see* 33:17,18,24). The young comforter continues by telling Job how good and just God is. God will never afflict man unless he deserves it. "For he will not lay upon man more than right; that he should enter into judgment with God" (34:23). So, in his final comforting word Elihu, though less blunt, still maintains God is just and Job is unrighteous.

The Response of Job

The context of the Book of Job, after the speech of Elihu, has God speak. We shall note some of the things He asks Job. But before we do this, and since we are dealing with the high points of this great book, we shall return to the earlier chapters to examine some of the great responses that Job makes to his wretched comforters. He continually maintains his righteousness before God, and in so many words he says, "I am not inferior to you! I would reason with God! And as for you, let me say, if you were wise you would really shut up!" (*see* 13:1–5).

In pleading his case, Job feels that he needs a mediator who could bring him and God together, one who would understand them both. One of the high points in the Book of Job and in the entire Old Testament, is to be found here.

> For he is not a man as I am, that I should answer him, and we should come together in judgment. Neither is there any daysman, [redeemer—mediator] between us, that might lay his hand upon us both. Let him take his rod away from me, and let not his fear terrify me: Then would I speak, and not fear him; but it is not so with me.
>
> 9:32–35.

In this passage Job recognizes the holiness of God and a genuine sinfulness which is true of all men. But how can he please God if he doesn't know why he is suffering? He has tried to please God by living a blameless life. What else can he do? Affliction cannot be the result of sin in his case. He cannot go to court with God. Thus he cries for a mediator.

We must keep in mind that Job lived before the coming of the Saviour-Mediator. How blessed we are on this side of the cross. We have the Mediator who pleads for us at the right hand of the

Heavenly Father (Romans 8:34). Paul speaks of this Mediator to young Timothy. Christ is the Mediator between man and God (1 Timothy 2:5,6).

Job does not doubt God, as did Jeremiah, nor does he complain to God, as did Moses. He only wants to know *why* he suffers. If there is something he has left undone, he wants to please God by doing it. This is declared by Job in the tenth chapter. "Why do you condemn me? Why do you contend with me? How can you reject me, I am yours!" (*see* 10:2,3). In his searching questions, Job shows that he has gained great spiritual insight as he has walked with his God. The peak of Job's faith is found in the nineteenth chapter of his book. Physically, Job is dying. His body is being consumed by its putrid sores. As he approaches death, he looks forward to his resurrection and life everlasting. Hear him!

> For I know that my redeemer liveth, and that he shall stand at the latter day upon the earth: And though after my skin worms destroy this body, yet in my flesh shall I see God: Whom I shall see for myself, and mine eyes shall behold, and not another; though my reins be consumed within me!
>
> 19:25–27

As Satan heard this witness of courage, confidence, and hope, he could not help but know that Job served the Lord because he loved Him, not for what he could get from Him, as he had charged.

We now come to the important question: Suffering such affliction, and being made so wretched by his comforters, what was it that enabled Job to have such faith? How could he rest in God's sovereignty when he could not understand what was happening to him?

Job knew the art of biblical thinking, which made him strong in his Lord. He did not know the reason for what was happening, God did! He knew he could not change God's mind, he knew his life was in God's hands. He also knew that God had his welfare in His heart. He knew these things from God's unchanging Word. Let him tell us:

> But he knoweth the way that I take: when he hath tried me, I shall come forth as gold. My foot hath held his steps, his ways have I kept, and not declined [gone back]. Neither have I gone back from the commandment of his lips; I have esteemed the words of his mouth more than my necessary food. But he is of one mind, and who can turn him? and what his soul desireth, even that he doeth. For he performeth the thing that is appointed for me: and many such things are with him.
>
> Job 23:10–14

As biblical thinking greatly influenced Paul, Moses and Jeremiah, so has God's Word influenced Job.

The Response of God

The men have spoken; now God speaks. He asks Job a number of startling questions which cause Job and the men to see that they are but creatures; God alone is the Creator. He alone is God Almighty.

A sample of these questions will suffice. "Where were you when I created the world?" (*see* 38:4–7). "Have you, as a man, been able to conquer death? Has its gates been open to you, or are you still in its shadow?" (*see* 38:17). "Have you managed to apply the laws of heaven to the kingdoms of men?" (*see* 38:33). "What can you tell the Almighty He doesn't already know?" (*see* 40:2). Who can answer God? Job decides to keep silence (*see* 40:3–6). Job cannot answer God, neither can he change His mind. He acknowledges that he is but a man and that God is truly God (*see* 42:4,5).

By this the test is ended. There is no record that Job ever learned of the contest between God and Satan as the first two chapters of the book present it to us. This may be so Job would live by faith and not by sight. This too, may be the reason why we also do not know all the answers to questions such as, "Why do the righteous suffer?" From our study we have seen that a strong faith can withstand the physical and mental afflictions which we are called upon to experience. We learn again that the source of a strong faith is to be rooted and grounded in God's Word, so we can develop a biblical mind set through biblical thinking. Thus, when a crisis comes we can take it in stride instead of stumbling into confusion, wretchedness, and fear.

After speaking to Job, God addresses Eliphaz and the other comforters. He rebukes them for the things they said to Job and vindicates His servant before them. ". . . for ye have not spoken of me the thing that is right, as my servant Job hath" (42:7). The comforters offer a burnt offering sacrifice at God's bidding, and He has Job pray for them. Then God restores to Job double that which he had lost, for the faithfulness of Job has vindicated God in the eyes of Satan. There are those who do love God for what He is, not for what they can get from Him.

We too shall be subject to all the pressures which Job experienced. Our Lord assures us of this (*see* John 16:33). However, we have in Christ a Mediator who is at the throne of grace interceding for us (*see* Romans 8:34). Doubtless, had it been written, Job would have sung as we can now:

> O for a faith that will not shrink,
> Tho pressed by many a foe,
> That will not tremble on the brink
> Of any earthly woe.
>
> That will not murmur nor complain
> Beneath the chast'ning rod,

But in the hour of grief or pain
Will lean upon its God;

Lord, give me such a faith as this,
And then, what-e'ere may come,
I'll taste, e'en now, the hallowed bliss
Of an eternal home.

WILLIAM H. BATHURST

7

The Power of Arrogant Thinking

"PRIDE GOETH BEFORE a fall," says the old proverb. Indeed it does, and carries much destruction in its wake. Lucifer thought he might be God as well as a mere creature, and fell from heaven. Eve thought she would do her husband a favor, and partook of the forbidden fruit which would have made them like God. As a result, they were made exiles of the Garden of Eden and missed the privilege of managing the earth for God. And down through the human race, pride has continued on its destructive way.

Though pride may be the sin of sins, it has many different forms. A gifted person may not realize that his abilities have been given to him by his Creator. Ignoring the fact, he looks down upon the less fortunate with scorn and disdain. Another person may have become arrogant as the result of being spoiled during his childhood. His parents and companions have let him have his way, and now, though a man, he is immature and selfish. He has to dominate everything and everyone he meets. He keeps everyone in a hostile mood, and it is not long before the group of which he is a part disintegrates.

Even in Christian communities proud thinking can be very destructive. A man of wealth seeks to dominate the church of which he is a member. Members of a church who are interrelated through marriage try to run the business of the church and are indifferent to the views of the other members when problems are discussed. What is true of churches can be true in other social groups as well.

Even in the group of twelve disciples, the Lord had to contend with sinful pride. When the disciples thought Jesus had come to be Messiah instead of the Saviour, they looked forward to prominent positions in the Kingdom. James and John wanted the chief seats beside the Lord. They did not have the courage to ask him outright, so they sent their mother to make the request. Judas would betray Him. And as we shall soon see, Peter will deny Him. All were disappointed in Him (*see* John 14:28–30).

Of the disciples, Peter proves to be one of the most interesting, impulsive, and proud. He was the ''Joe Blow'' of the group. Even when he had nothing to say he managed to say it. He would be the leader of the group, acting on impulse. At the same time, he showed elements of great spiritual insight. Yet he was stubborn, his attitude seemed to be, ''Why learn anything the easy way if it can be learned the hard way.'' So he learned it the hard way.

As we study the life of Peter we shall examine the nature of his arrogance, how it led to his denial of his Lord, and then, having gone through great hardship, he will give us a testimony of the precious faith and promises which he found in the Saviour. Peter may well have been a problem to his Saviour, but when the Bible conquered him, he gave us two great epistles, so we can learn from his experiences.

The Arrogance of Peter

Peter was a well-meaning leader, but it was his pride and impulsiveness that got him into trouble. It was his brother Andrew who brought him to the Lord. The Saviour looked not only *at* him but *into* him as well. He recognized the man's weaknesses, but told him He would transform his life (*see* John 1:40–42). Andrew and Peter doubtless told Philip of their experience, and Philip became a follower of Christ (John 1:43,44).

Peter always had an answer when a question was asked. On one occasion, the Lord asked His disciples as to whom men thought He was. Various answers were given. Some thought He was John the

Baptist; others thought He was Elijah; some mistook Him for Jeremiah, or one of the prophets. When Jesus asked them who they thought He was, Peter was ready with the answer. "And Simon Peter answered and said, Thou art the Christ, the Son of the living God. And Jesus answered and said unto him, Blessed art thou, Simon Bar-jonah: for flesh and blood hath not revealed it unto thee, but my Father which is in heaven" (Matthew 16:16,17). Thus the Lord commends him for his spiritual insight, but a few verses later the Saviour has to rebuke him because of his impulsiveness. We read:

> From that time forth began Jesus to show unto his disciples, how that he must go unto Jerusalem, and suffer many things of the elders and the chief priests and scribes, and be killed, and be raised again the third day. Then Peter took him, and began to rebuke him, saying, Be it far from thee, Lord: this shall not be unto thee. But he turned, and said unto Peter, Get thee behind me, Satan: thou art an offense unto me: for thou savourest not of the things that be of God, but those that be of men.
>
> Matthew 16:21–23

In his crazy way, Peter was well-meaning, no doubt, but was impulsively foolish. To correct the Lord is a matter of silly brashness. These two incidents show the volatile character of this devoted disciple. Peter would save his Lord, but it is Peter who has to be saved.

If Peter had been only impulsive he might have saved himself a lot of trouble, but along with his impulsiveness there was pride as well. We find ourselves at the Last Supper. Jesus told his disciples that one of them would betray Him. He hints that He is now on the way to the cross and that they will not be able to follow Him. Peter, who is accustomed to correcting the Lord, does it again.

Little children, yet a little while I am with you. Ye shall seek me and as I said unto the Jews, Whither I go ye cannot come; so now I say to you. . . . Simon Peter said unto him, Lord, whither goest thou? Jesus answered him, Whither I go, thou canst not follow me now; but thou shalt follow me afterwards. Peter said unto him, Lord, why cannot I follow thee now? I will lay down my life for thy sake. Jesus answered him, Wilt thou lay down thy life for my sake? Verily, verily, I say unto thee, The cock shall not crow, till thou hast denied me thrice.

John 13:33,36–38

As we turn to the account of this event in the Gospel of Luke, we are told of a prayer which our Lord prays which will not be answered. The disciples are fighting among themselves as to who should be honored as the greatest in the Kingdom of Heaven. The Lord rebukes them and informs them that he who serves shall be accounted the greatest in the Kingdom (*see* Luke 22:24–30). Then He says to Peter, calling him by the name that speaks of his weakness:

And the Lord said, Simon, Simon, behold, Satan hath desired to have you, that he may sift you as wheat: But I have prayed for thee, that thy faith fail not: and when thou art converted, [brought back into fellowship] strengthen thy brethren.

Luke 22:31,32

Matthew, in his account, gives us that detail which manifests the arrogance of Peter.

Then saith Jesus unto them, All ye shall be offended because of me this night: for it is written, I will smite the shepherd, and the sheep of the flock shall be scattered abroad. But after I am risen again, I will go before you into Galilee. Peter answered and said unto him, Though all men shall be offended because of thee, yet will I never be offended.

Matthew 26:31–33

And upon this boast, the Lord reminded Peter that he would deny Him.

Could the Lord pray a prayer that was not answered? If so, why did He pray such a prayer? His desire was to save Peter the agony of denying Him. In this sense it was not answered. He also prayed that Peter would learn from the tragedy that was to befall him. In this sense His prayer was answered. You and I will pray such prayers for people who can only learn by breaking their heads and learning the hard way. Some people cannot take advice. Before surrendering to God's will they have to be broken by it.

The Denials of Peter

Before we consider the denials of Peter, there is another phase of his character we should consider. Though Peter did some dumb things, yet he truly loved his Lord. We can say even his denial of the Lord was not born of hatred and greed, as that of Judas, but rather of fear. We see the disciple's love for his Lord in the following incident. The Saviour was facing a crisis in His ministry. He spoke of His spiritual kingdom which He came to establish. This brought great sorrow to His followers. Many began to leave Him. He knew those who believed in Him and those who did not. As many turned away from Him, we read, "Then said Jesus unto the twelve, Will ye also go away? Then Simon Peter answered him, Lord, to whom shall we go? thou hast the words of eternal life. And we believe and are sure that thou art the Christ, the Son of the living God" (John 6:67–69). Impulsive? Yes! Absolutely certain? Yes! Speaking for the others? True! But with a heart of devotion, even though Peter may not have considered the cost. Let us not forget, biblical thinking grows out of the "words of eternal life."

Peter's denial of his Lord grows out of fear. Peter is no longer the professed defender of his Lord. As an observer of the trials of the Saviour, he follows from afar. Then he warms himself at the enemies' fire, which is no place to be when he should be at his Saviour's side. A maid recognizes Peter and tells the men that this man is Christ's disciple. Peter calls the maid a liar and denies that he ever knew Christ. Another in the crowd, a little while later, sees Peter and accuses him of being a follower of Christ. Quite heatedly Peter denies it. An hour later, a third person accuses Peter of being a Galilean. The man is very sure about it. Peter replies that he doesn't know what the man is saying (*see* Luke 22:54–60).

Four things now happen: while Peter was making his third denial, the cock crowed, the Lord turned and looked at Peter, Peter remembered the word of the Lord, he went out and wept bitterly (Luke 22:60–62). How could he stand there as the godless men mocked and struck the Lord who loved him?

Of the eleven disciples, who has the most miserable time between the times of Christ's trial and crucifixion and the resurrection? There can be no doubt, it is Peter. He thought he loved his Lord. He had told Him so. What went wrong? How could he deny the One who had prayed for him? The tale is told. Some time later, after the resurrection, the disciples spend a night fishing. They fish all the night and catch nothing. As usual, Peter is the ringleader (*see* John 21:3). In the morning, the disciples see a figure on the beach, but they do not recognize Him. He calls across the water to ask if they have caught any fish. They haven't. He instructs them where to cast their nets, and to their surprise they draw a large catch. John, the beloved disciple, recognizes the figure on the shore to be the Lord. Impulsive Peter throws his cloak about him and dives into the water for the shore. The other disciples follow in the boat. They reach the shore and bring the fish to land. None of the disciples dare ask Him if He is the Lord. They know He is; they wish He weren't. There is some unsettled business to be taken care of.

The Lord bids them come and have breakfast with Him. The risen Christ takes fish and bread and serves His seven disciples. Thus the story so far (*see* John 21:3–14). One question, repeated three times, is now asked by the Lord to Peter. "Do you love (*agapao*) me more than these?" Who are the "these?" Could it possibly be the other disciples (*see* Matthew 26:33)? Peter had said that they might be offended in Him, but he would not be. Could it be the fish? Peter lived by the water. Fishing was to him what golf is to many men of our day (*see* John 21:3). To the first and second questions "Do you love me more than these?" Peter answers, "Thou knowest that I *like* (*phileo*) thee." The Lord seemingly takes no notice to the term *like* as opposed to the word *love*. In each answer of Peter's the Lord bids him feed His sheep. There is a change in the third question.

He saith unto him the third time, Simon, son of Jonas, likest thou me [do you only like me]? Peter was grieved because he said unto him the third time Likest thou me? And he said unto him, Lord, thou knowest all things, thou knowest that I only like thee. Jesus said unto him, Feed my sheep.

see John 21:17

What more was there to say? People know whether they *love* or *like* the Lord, even though their vocabulary may be misleading. Christ knows the difference between *love* and *like,* not only in the meaning of words but in the meaning of the heart as well.

Peter may have only *liked* the Lord, but he had abundant proof that the Lord *loved* him. On the morning of the resurrection, what is in the Lord's mind? Mark records it for us. The holy women come to the tomb on that early morning so long ago. They wonder who will remove the stone from the tomb's entrance. To their amazement the stone is rolled away. A young man sitting in the open tomb tells them that Jesus is risen. He adds "But go your way and tell his disciples and Peter that he goeth before you into Galilee: there shall ye see him, as he said unto you" (Mark 16:7). "And Peter!" Though he denied Jesus, our Lord did not forget him. No one can measure the love of Christ. No wonder Peter was grieved when he really learned that he only *liked* the Lord who *loved* him.

The Witness of Peter

Peter remembered the words of the Lord. In his witness through his epistles we can see how precious this tragic experience became to him. He who was a coward before the Lord's enemies became bold to declare him as the Book of the Acts attests (*see* 2:14–36). In his epistles he speaks of "precious faith" (*see* 1 Peter 1:6,7). He makes reference to "precious blood" (1:18–20). Then he makes references to the fact that God's faithfulness and promises are "precious" (*see* 2 Peter 1:1,4). Peter, when speaking of trials, speaks from experience. Trials are used by the Lord to purify us. The slag of carnality is removed from the true ore (*see* 1 Peter 1:6,7). And the apostle's letters show that he has profited from his sad experience. The blood of Christ is precious because it tells us how God, before the foundation of the world, would have to send His Son as Saviour, if lost men whom He knew would wreck His world, were to be saved (1 Peter 1:18–20). Peter would join Paul in declaring, "If God be for us, who can be against us?" (Romans 8:31). Doubtless Peter thanked God for the rooster who sounded the note that turned him to remember the Word and come back to his Lord.

Proud, foolish, impulsive, but a victim of grace. This was the experience of Peter. He learned to love his Lord the hard way. His farewell word to us is from the heart, and not from his head.

Simon Peter, a servant and an apostle of Jesus Christ, to them that have obtained like precious faith with us through the righteousness of God and our Saviour Jesus Christ: Grace and peace be multiplied unto you through the knowledge of God, and of Jesus our Lord, According as his divine power hath given unto us all things that pertain unto life and godliness, through the knowledge of him that hath called us to glory and virtue: Whereby are given unto us exceeding great and precious promises: that by these we might be partakers of the divine nature, having escaped the corruption that is in the world through lust.

2 Peter 1:1–4

It is these "precious promises" that changed the life of Peter. These promises are to be found in God's Word, and it is the Word of God that enables us to think biblically so that we too who are proud, foolish, and impulsive may come to love the Lord instead of just "liking" Him. And with Peter we can sing:

> Loved with everlasting love,
> Led by grace that love to know—
> Spirit, breathing from above,
> Thou hast taught me it is so!
> O this full and perfect peace
> O this transport all divine—
> In a love which cannot cease,
> I am His, and He is mine.
>
> His forever, only His—
> Who the Lord and me shall part?
> Ah, with what a rest of bliss
> Christ can fill the loving heart!
> Heav'n and earth may fade and flee,
> First-born light in gloom decline,
> But, while God and I shall be,
> I am His, and He is mine.

WADE ROBINSON

8

The Power of Lustful Thinking

MAN, BECAUSE OF his sinful nature, has the habit of living a double life. In his public life, he tries to live a life of goodness and respectability. In his private life, he grows careless and many times his conduct leaves something to be desired. As long as he has self-respect, he endeavors to keep these two phases of his life apart. However, the sinfulness of man is more powerful than the virtues he would manifest. Eventually what he is in his heart influences his mind and will, until his secret life becomes public property. Among the poor it is ignored. Among the great it becomes the occasion for scandal and juicy gossip. In our recent history, Watergate and the scandals of congressmen illustrate with a vengeance the Scriptural truth, ". . . be sure your sin will find you out" (Numbers 32:23). During the Watergate affair, James Reston, columnist for *The New York Times,* pointed out concerning "bugging" that the White House had nothing on God. In one of Reston's columns, he quoted the Gospel according to Luke, "For there is nothing covered, that shall not be revealed; neither hid, that shall not be known. Therefore whatsoever ye have spoken in darkness shall be heard in the light; and that which ye have spoken in the ear in closets, shall be proclaimed upon the housetops" (12:2,3).

In our past history, there have been other scandals among the high and low. Our moral climate then did not look with favor upon the transgressions of the mighty. Among all classes of people there was a respect for law and for one another's property. But since World War II, our country has been on a moral toboggan, and we have slid to the point where crime has become the order of the day. Congress finds it difficult to reform itself, and the only thing television can do is to turn the violent viciousness of men into profitable entertainment.

Man's greatest problem is the holiness of God. Because of His holiness, God refuses to allow man to get away with his unrighteous deeds. Man may consider himself sophisticated, mature, and relevant in our times as he looks upon evil as good and good as evil (*see* Isaiah 5:20,21). When man plays "hide & seek" with God, he soon learns that he is "it." Man can never succeed in being evil, for God has decreed that when His moral law is broken man will be broken too.

In the providence of God, man was created to be successful—to rule the world for Him. Only one condition was set for man to reach this goal. He was to be dependent upon God. In Adam, man prefers to be independent of God, and in his rebellious spirit tries to reach the goal of success without God. Without God, man has resorted to greed and lust to reach the goal which God had planned for him. Without God, man will never succeed, for the essence of sin is *to miss the mark*. God has decreed that the function of sin is to be "efficiently inefficient." No lesser man than Solomon found the truth of this statement from his own experience. "He that covereth his sins shall not prosper: but whoso confesseth and forsaketh them shall have mercy" (Proverbs 28:13). Young Elihu, in speaking to Job, sounds the same note. "For the work of a man shall he [God] render unto him, and cause every man to find according to his ways. Yea, surely God will not do wickedly, neither will the Almighty pervert judgment" (Job 34:11,12).

As we study the power of lustful thinking—which leads to a life of tragic destruction, we can do no better than to examine the life of Solomon, reputed to be the wisest man in all the world. He used his wisdom to become a fool. This brought him not only vexation of spirit, but eventually it brought him back to the God of his youth. He lived a public life of great devotion to his God, but his private life left much to be desired. It led to his ruin, which in turn made a shambles of the Kingdom of Israel. In God's grace, Solomon had the courage to leave us a record of his stupidity in order that we might see how a ruined man might again find blessing and hope in God. We shall learn that to live for self is ruinous, to live in the light of God's Law is prosperous.

The Prayer of Solomon

David, the great King of Israel has died. Solomon, his son, is now made king. Of him we read:

> And Solomon loved the LORD, walking in the statutes of David his father: only he sacrificed and burnt incense in high places. . . . In Gibeon, the LORD appeared to Solomon in a dream by night: and God said, Ask what I shall give thee.
>
> 1 Kings 3:3,5

There can be no doubt of the fact that Solomon began his reign on a high spiritual plane. He knew the responsibility of kingship. His great desire was to have the wisdom in order to rule his people well. Thus he made his request to God:

> Thou hast shewed unto thy servant David my father great mercy, according as he walked before thee in truth, and in righteousness, and in uprightness of heart with thee; and thou hast kept for him this great kindness, that thou hast given him a son to sit on his throne, as it is this day. And now, O LORD, my God, thou hast made thy servant king instead of David my father: and I am but a little child: I know not how to go out or come in. And thy servant is in the midst of thy people which thou hast chosen, a great people, that cannot be numbered, nor counted for multitude. Give therefore thy servant an under-

standing heart to judge thy people, that I may discern between good and bad: for who is able to judge this thy so great a people?

1 Kings 3:6–9

Before his death, King David had urged Solomon to be strong, to show himself a man, and to keep the Law of God in order that the blessing of God might be upon him. (*see* 1 Kings 2:2–4). According to the Law of Israel, the secret of blessing was to be in obedience to God and to serve Him with heart, soul, and mind (*see* Deuteronomy 6:4,5). Later, we shall see that God Himself urged Solomon to follow the advice of his royal father (*see* 1 Kings 9:4,5).

God recognizes the high spiritual tone of Solomon's request. The king's request pleased the Lord, for he did not ask anything for himself. He even did not make a request for God to slay his enemies. God would not only give him wisdom but make the king the greatest of all men in wisdom and in wealth (*see* 3:10–14).

What was the nature of the wisdom that Solomon requested? Was it the knowledge of facts? Was it the skill with which to rule his kingdom? Solomon was not interested in the head knowledge of the sophisticate, nor the art of compromise of the diplomat, but the heart knowledge of the heavenly Father. Of it he writes:

My son, if thou wilt receive my words, and hide my commandments with thee; So that thou incline thine ear unto wisdom, and apply thine heart to understanding; Yea, if thou criest after knowledge, and liftest up thy voice for understanding; If thou seekest her as silver, and searchest for her as for hid treasures; Then shalt thou understand the fear of the LORD, and find the knowledge of God. For the LORD giveth wisdom: out of his mouth cometh knowledge and understanding. He layeth up sound wisdom for the righteous: he is a buckler to them that walk uprightly. He keepeth the paths of judgment, and preserveth the way of his saints. Then shalt thou understand righteousness, and judgment, and equity; yea, every good path.

Proverbs 2:1–9

Indeed, this was good, godly wisdom which Solomon needed to rule his people well. Israel had fallen upon evil days. Because of the defection of the priesthood, the children of Israel had become indifferent to the ways of the Lord. Each man did that which was right in his own eyes (*see* Judges 21:25). A number of the great judges, strong in character, tried to bring the people back to God, but upon their death, the people returned to their old sinful ways. God granted Solomon his request (*see* 1 Kings 3:10–14), and in the beginning of his reign, the king walked in the ways of the Lord and became known for his great wisdom, his greatness of heart, and his fame was known throughout the whole eastern world (*see* 4:29–31). He also experienced the time of peace which God had promised for him to his father, David (*see* 1 Chronicles 22:9). Thus he was able to bring order out of Israel's moral, political, and religious confusion.

The Devotion of Solomon

One of the great desires of King David was to build a suitable house for God. Up to his time, God made His presence known in the Tabernacle, a portable tent which could be carried about as the people were traveling through the wilderness. But now, in the Promised Land, where the people had settled, the king thought that a permanent home for Israel's God was in order. David was not given this privilege. King Solomon has the honor to build a Temple for the God of Israel (*see* 1 Chronicles 22:6–16). Thus Solomon sets to work to build the Temple for the Lord as one of the first acts of his reign. (1 Kings 5:3–5).

In the building of the Temple, no expense is spared. It becomes an architectural masterpiece. It takes seven years and six months to build God's house (*see* 1 Kings 6:1, 37,38), and when it is finished all the things that David had prepared for it are placed within it by his son, Solomon (*see* 1 Kings 7:51). During its building, God promises Solomon that He will dwell in it.

> And the word of the LORD came to Solomon, saying, Concerning this house which thou art in building, if thou wilt walk in my statutes, and execute my judgments, and keep all my commandments to walk in them; then will I perform my word with thee, which I spake unto David thy father: And I will dwell among the children of Israel, and will not forsake my people Israel. So Solomon built the house, and finished it.
>
> 1 Kings 6:11–14

The day of dedication dawns. The people and the priests are gathered before the Temple. Great sacrifices are offered. The priests begin their various ministries. The elders of the people are assembled. The Ark of the Covenant is brought to the Temple and placed within the Holy of Holies (1 Kings 8:1–11). The Lord makes His presence known as the glory cloud fills the Temple. Solomon then acknowledges the Lord's acceptance of His house.

> Then spake Solomon, the LORD said that he would dwell in the thick darkness. I have surely built thee an house to dwell in, a settled place for thee to abide in for ever. And the king turned his face about, and blessed all the congregation of Israel: (and all the congregation of Israel stood;) And he said, Blessed be the LORD God of Israel, which spake with his mouth unto David my father, and hath with his hand fulfilled it, saying, Since the day that I brought forth my people Israel out of Egypt, I chose no city out of all the tribes of Israel to build an house, that my name might be therein; but I chose

David to be over my people Israel. And it was in the heart of David my father to build an house for the name of the LORD God of Israel. And the LORD said unto David my father, Whereas it was in thine heart to build an house unto my name, thou didst well that it was in thine heart. Nevertheless, thou shalt not build the house; but thy son who shalt come forth out of thy loins, he shall build the house unto my name. And the LORD hath performed his word that he spake, and I am risen up in the room of David my father, and sit on the throne of Israel, as the LORD promised, and have built an house for the name of the LORD God of Israel. And I have set there a place for the ark, wherein is the covenant of the LORD, which he made with our fathers, when he brought them out of the land of Egypt.

1 Kings 8:12–21

Then Solomon offers his great prayer of dedication (*see* 1 Kings 8:22–54). He rejoices in God's faithfulness to him, to his father David, and to the children of Israel. The King prays that God will hear the prayers of His children. If they sin and come to know His judgment, may He be forgiving if they repent and return to Him. Above all, Solomon trusts that as God's children, they will walk in His ways.

In this prayer of dedication, Solomon makes a great theological point which modern day theologians have not solved. If God is omnipresent—everywhere—how can He be in one local place? God solved the problem, though theologians haven't! Hear Solomon raise the question:

But will God indeed dwell on the earth? behold, the heaven and the heaven of heavens cannot contain thee; how much less this house that I have builded? Yet, have thou respect unto the prayer of thy servant, and to his supplication, O LORD my

God, to hearken unto the cry and the prayer, which thy servant prayeth before thee to day: That thine eyes may be open toward this house night and day, even toward the place of which thou hast said, My name shall be there: that thou mayest hearken unto the prayer which thy servant shall make toward this place. And hearken thou unto the supplication of thy servant, and of thy people Israel, when they shall pray toward this place: and hear thou in heaven thy dwelling place: and when thou hearest, forgive.

1 Kings 8:27–30

God is everywhere as God, but as the heavenly Father who cares for His children He is with them personally. The mystery of *how* is His; The blessing *that it is,* is ours.

Solomon is wise, great, powerful, renowned. But God does not let him forget that he is His servant. After the celebration of dedication, God promises to bless Solomon if he will walk in His way; He promises to curse Solomon and Israel if they become disobedient and rebellious, disregarding the statutes and judgment of the Law. (*see* 1 Kings 9:1–9).

The Queen of Sheba hears of Solomon's fame but does not believe what she hears. She has to come and see for herself. She pays a visit to the royal court and the Temple and is amazed by what she sees. "The half has not been told," she exclaims. Then she asks God's blessing upon the king, his servants, and the children of Israel. She presents him with gifts worthy of his station (*see* 1 Kings 10:1–11). The Queen returns to her own country with gifts which she receives from Solomon.

The Stupidity of Solomon

How is it possible for a wise king who loves God, who builds a great Temple for His God, to turn out to be such a fool that through lust he destroys himself, and through his sin destroys his kingdom? We might ask a further question: since Solomon did so many wonderful things for his people and for God Himself, couldn't God be a little less severe in His judgment of Solomon? When one of our great leaders falls from high office because of his evil deeds, we search for his good deeds to counterbalance his evil ones. This allows us to show him some respect at least. The answer to the second question is that God differs from us. He is absolutely holy and His judgment is just. We are sinful and are not in the position for "the pot to call the kettle black!" The first question has an answer too. Solomon *just about* loved the Lord, and *just about* walked in His ways. We say *just about,* for he had made an alliance with Egypt and had married one of Pharaoh's daughters (1 Kings 3:1,3). The Law clearly forbade this (*see* Deuteronomy 17:15–20). To look to other nations to help Israel in her trouble, would cause Israel to depend upon man instead of God. For the children of Israel to marry foreign women would lead to idolatry on the part of Israel. In his private life, Solomon planted the seed of rebellion. During his public life, the seed of sin took root and began to grow until it reached full flower. We get a glimpse of its growth, for while Solomon is building a house for God, he is building one for himself as well. He also builds a house for his Egyptian wife (*see* 1 Kings 7:1,8). By the time we come to the eleventh chapter of First Kings, Solomon's secret sin breaks through into his public life and God's judgment begins to operate.

But King Solomon loved many strange women, together with the daughter of Pharaoh, women of the Moabites, the Ammonites, the Edomites, the Zidonians, and Hittites; Of the nations concerning which the LORD said unto the children of Israel, Ye shall not go in to them, neither shall they come in unto you: for surely they will turn away your heart after their gods: Solomon clave unto these in love. And he had seven hundred wives, princesses, and three hundred concubines: and his wives turned away his heart. For it came to pass, when

Solomon was old, that his wives turned away his heart after other gods: and his heart was not perfect [blameless] with the LORD his God, as was the heart of David his father.

1 Kings 11:1–4

Solomon builds shrines to the gods of his wives. Probably, it seemed better to him to keep peace with them than with God. Lustful thinking has a way of taking God for granted. But God will not be taken for granted. Judgment comes soon and severely. God is angry with Solomon. Not only does Solomon sin against God, his influence is such that it is not long before the nation follows his example. God appears to the king and tells him of the judgment which is to fall upon him and his kingdom.

And the LORD was angry with Solomon, because his heart was turned from the LORD God of Israel, which had appeared unto him twice. And had commanded him concerning this thing, that he should not go after other gods: but he kept not that which the LORD commanded. Wherefore the LORD said unto Solomon, Forasmuch as this is done of thee, and thou hast not kept my covenant, and my statutes, which I have commanded thee, I will surely rend the kingdom from thee, and will give it to thy servant. Notwithstanding in thy days I will not do it for David thy father's sake: but I will rend it out of the hand of thy son. Howbeit I will not rend away all the kingdom; but will give one tribe to thy son for David my servant's sake, and for Jerusalem's sake which I have chosen.

1 Kings 11:9–13

After pronouncing His judgment, God stirs up adversaries against Solomon, and the rest of the king's days are filled with grief and wretchedness. Jeroboam rebels against his royal master and will be the one to lead ten of the tribes away from Solomon's son to form the Northern Kingdom. Rehoboam, Solomon's son, will make this possible through his own stupidity, by levying upon the people more taxes than they can bear (*see* 1 Kings 12:1–24). The power of lustful thinking leads not only to personal tragedy, but its influence can lead to the destruction of a family, a society, and in Solomon's case, a nation as well. For Israel and Judah, the names by which the divided nation was known, never recovered from the judgment which God brought upon Solomon and his people.

The Advice of Solomon

Solomon was not only great in wisdom, and as we have just seen, great in stupidity; he was also great in confession and repentance as well. He externalized his sin in confession, and gave us a record of his repentance. Solomon *could* write good theology— even orthodox theology, and know it only in theory. He *doesn't* do that! He writes from experience, "He that covereth his sins shall not prosper: but whoso confesseth and forsaketh them shall have mercy" (Proverbs 28:13). Many of our great men when their sins are discovered would rather go to hell arrogantly than confess to God and in His mercy go to heaven humbly. In the Proverbs and in the Book of Ecclesiastes, we can trace the line of Solomon's meditations and adopt his advice if lustful thinking destroys us as it did him.

There can be no doubt that when Solomon returned to his senses from his lust for wealth and women, he found the peace which mercy brings when sin is confessed. From experience he could agree with Isaiah, "But the wicked are like the troubled sea, when it cannot rest, whose waters cast up mire and dirt. There is no peace, saith my God, to the wicked" (57:20,21). Let us listen to Solomon in his restless, wretched state.

Life is a weariness when men serve themselves:

All things are full of labour; man cannot utter it: the eye is not satisfied with seeing, nor the ear filled with hearing. The thing that hath been, it is that which shall be; and that which is done is that which shall be done: and there is no new thing under the sun.

Ecclesiastes 1:8,9

Life is difficult without God:

I, the Preacher, was king over Israel in Jerusalem, and I gave my heart to seek and search out by wisdom concerning all things that are done under heaven: this sore travail hath God given to the sons of man to be exercised therewith. I have seen all the works that are done under the sun; and, behold, all is vanity and vexation of spirit. That which is crooked cannot be made straight: and that which is wanting cannot be numbered. I communed with mine own heart, saying, Lo, I am come to great estate, and have gotten more wisdom than all they that have been before me in Jerusalem: yea, my heart had great experience of wisdom and knowledge. And I gave my heart to know wisdom, and to know madness and folly: I perceived that this also is vexation of spirit. For in much wisdom is much grief: and he that increaseth knowledge increaseth sorrow.

Ecclesiastes 1:12–18

Man must come to grips with God:

He [God] hath made every thing beautiful in his time: also he hath set the worlds [eternity, ages] in their heart, so that no man can find out the work that God maketh from the beginning to the end. I know that there is no good in them, but for a man to rejoice, and to do good in his life. And also that every man should eat and drink, and enjoy the good of all his labour, it is the gift of God. I know that, whatsoever God doeth, it shall be for ever: nothing can be put to it, nor any thing taken from it: and God doeth it, that men should fear [have regard for] before him. That which hath been is now; and that which is to be hath already been; and God requireth that which is past.

And moreover I saw under the sun the place of judgment, that wickedness was there; and the place of righteousness, that iniquity was there. I said in mine heart, God shall judge the righteous and the wicked: for there is a time there for every purpose and for every work. I said in mine heart concerning the estate of the sons of men, that God might manifest them and that they might see that they themselves are beasts.

Ecclesiastes 3:11–18

Youth should not forget their Creator if they would avoid a bitter old age:

Remember now thy Creator in the days of thy youth, while the evil days come not, nor the years draw nigh, when thou shalt say, I have no pleasure in them; While the sun, or the light, or the moon, or the stars, be not darkened, nor the clouds return after the rain. . . . And further, by these, my son, be admonished: of the making of many books there is no end; and much study is a weariness of the flesh.

Let us hear the conclusion of the whole matter: Fear God and keep his commandments: for this is the whole duty of man. For God shall bring every work into judgment, with every secret thing, whether it be good, or whether it be evil.

Ecclesiastes 12:1,2,12–14

We have said previously that man's greatest problem is God's holiness. Solomon would add: "And along with His holiness is His sovereignty as well!" God loved Solomon too much to destroy him. He loved him enough not to spoil him—to let him get away with his lustful thoughts. He loved him enough to have this great king feel the rigors of judgment which would drive him back to his God. And Solomon had the good sense to return to his God, to know His forgiveness, and to experience His mercy.

A close study of the above citations will show us that what was true in the time of Solomon is just as true today. Whether one's lust is for power, or greatness, or wealth, or women (or men), or for whatever it may be, to ignore God is to be in trouble. As the wise old king tells us, "Everything under the sun leads only to weariness and vexation of spirit. Everything is vanity of vanities—in the Hebrew sense—everything is futile" (*see* Ecclesiastes 1:14). Space doesn't allow us to give Solomon's complete thought. To read the Book of Proverbs and the Book of Ecclesiastes will gives us his full thought on the subject. He comes to the conclusion that there is no justice. History repeats itself. Man cannot escape God, for He has planted eternity in their hearts (*see* Ecclesiastes 3:11). To avoid bitterness and wretchedness in old age, the only thing to do is to come to know God in your youth, and then don't forget Him in your lifetime.

Solomon's Sin Solution

Reader, you and I can avoid the pitfalls which Solomon encountered if we realize that we are prone to the same stupidities that he experienced. We too can be the victims of our base desires, not only in the sexual world, but in the world of power and fame. The world believes that "power corrupts." Solomon and the Bible would disagree. It is we who corrupt power. Power and desire are useful things when put to just and righteous uses. It is sinful man that abuses desire and power. He corrupts them; they do not corrupt him. And it is interesting to note in proving the point, that God holds man responsible for what he does with desire and power; God does not hold these inanimate things responsible.

To come back to God and confess his sin brought Solomon the godly peace which he had lost. To cover his sin was to know adversity. To confess it was to know forgiveness and mercy. To you who have read these pages, God sent Christ to die on Calvary that mercy might be shown to you. He arose from the dead, ascended into heaven, and now intercedes for those who might be as wretched as Solomon. There was a time that our past brought us to the place of lonely, restless wretchedness. Our hearts were like the "troubled sea" of the prophet Isaiah. Then there came a change. We turned to Christ, even as Solomon turned to the God of his father David. One of our hymns expresses it well:

> I've tried in vain a thousand ways
> My fears to quell, my hopes to raise;
> But what I need, the Bible says,
> Is ever, only Jesus.
>
> My soul is night, my heart is steel—
> I cannot see, I cannot feel;
> For light, for life, I must appeal
> In simple faith to Jesus.
>
> He died, He lives, He reigns, He pleads;
> There's love in all His words and deeds;
> There's all a guilty sinner needs
> Forever more in Jesus.
>
> Though some should sneer; and some should blame;
> I'll go with all my guilt and shame;
> I'll go to Him, because His name,
> Above all names is Jesus.
>
> JAMES PROCTOR

Remember the admonition of Solomon: ". . . he who confesseth and forsaketh his sins shall have mercy" (*see* Proverbs 28:13).

9

The Power
of Persistent Thinking

HAVING STUDIED the power of positive, negative, transformed, and faithful thinking, we now consider the power of persistent thinking. For there are times when this mode of thinking is necessary if one is to be a success. So often people who should be a help to one are not. Their advice is discouraging or lacking, their criticism is plentiful. To the persistent thinker, ''Never say die!'' is the watchword. Because they must fight their way to success, persistent people can be obnoxious to the negative and slothful thinkers. Because of being rebuffed and discouraged by others, they have the tendency to disregard their fellows in order to reach their goal. Nevertheless, if it were not for their persistent thinking, they would not be the great leaders they turn out to be.

There are several accounts of persistent thinkers in the Bible. Some expressed their thoughts in terms of prayer. Others kept asking questions until the answer for which they were searching was given to them. And there is even an instance where a woman of Canaan was rebuffed by the Lord, and they began to play ''Can You Top This?'' so it seems. As a result the woman displayed great faith, and the Saviour answered her question and made her daughter whole. We shall discuss this event in a moment. It was my favorite story in the Scriptures even before I was saved, for I had read the Bible several times because I deemed it to be good literature. One Sunday afternoon, however, I tuned in the radio to hear a voice telling this story. It was that of the late Dr. Donald Grey Barn-house. Later, he came to our city. I went to hear him, and through his ministry I came to know the Lord.

There are at least two types of persistent thinking which are dangerous that which is born of stubbornness and the other which is born of credulity—foolish faith which is nothing more than wishful thinking. Stubbornness can lead to destruction. A person without foresight and ability can persist in undertaking a project which demands both of these qualities. To persist without these attributes, and to disregard the advice of friends is bound to lead to failure. In the religious realm, this type of stubbornness is manifested many times in misplaced faith. What God has done for some is no guarantee that He will do the same for all. The Scriptures are careful to show that faith is not a matter of ignorance. There are credentials that biblical faith demands, not only in a subjective sense, but in an objective sense as well. We are not bidden to believe blindly. In every instance where faith is concerned God gives us sufficient facts upon which to rest our faith. We shall see this as we study the essence of persistent thinking.

In this chapter we want to discover the nature of persistent thinking in the realm of faith. We shall look for three things: What is the basis of persistent thinking? What are the hindrances to persistent thinking? How can intelligent, persistent thinking be demonstrated?

The Basis of Persistent Thinking

We find ourselves again involved in the art of biblical thinking, which relates us to persistent thinking, leading us to the doctrine of biblical faith. When considering persistent thinking in the secular realm, it stands to reason that belief and trust play an important part in the process of persistence. One must believe that there is a goal to reach and he must trust his abilities and circumstances to reach the goal. In biblical thinking we must see what God's Word says about faith. Not only is there the question of belief on our part, but also what are we to believe insofar as God is concerned.

As to our own faith, we must believe that there is a God in whom we can trust, and that as we trust Him, He will make Himself known to us. The writer to the Hebrews makes this quite clear, "But without faith it is impossible to please him: for he that cometh to God must believe that he is, and that he is a rewarder of them that diligently seek him" (Hebrews 11:6). Here we are speaking in terms of subjective faith. It is the faith which we exercise when we say "I trust, I believe." But the verse moves one step further by hinting that there is an objective side of faith, as when we say, "Believe what! What shall I believe?" Our text reads that God will reward those who diligently seek Him. What is the nature of this reward?

In verse one of the eleventh chapter of the Epistle to the Hebrews, we read, "Now faith is the substance of things hoped for, the evidence of things not seen." This introduces us to a faith based upon some evidence which enables us to know whether our faith in God can be realized. A number of years ago, when living in the eastern part of our country, I had to go to our nation's capital. Mrs. Keiper had not been to Washington previously, but she was willing to drive me down from Philadelphia. To my surprise, she had no difficulty finding her way to the various places I wanted to visit. I asked her how she seemed to know the city so well. She replied, "You told me where you wanted to go. I consulted a map of the city and became familiar with the location of the various buildings and their relationship to one another. Having this in my mind, and checking the map, I had no difficulty finding my way." The Scriptures are our road map which gives us the *substance* of our faith and the *evidence* for our hope of realizing it. Had we disregarded the map, we would never have reached Washington; disregarding the Bible is but to find that that which we mistook for faith was only credulity.

Persistent thinking demands a steadfast faith. Had we questioned the veracity of the map, and every five miles had wondered if we had wandered on to the wrong road because of the map's possible inaccuracy, our trip would have been a nightmare and we might have never reached the District. But trusting the map, and submitting ourselves to it, the journey was filled with great pleasure as we accomplished all we set out to do. God warns us that we must trust His map, the Bible, if we are to receive blessings from Him. Our faith must not waver.

If any of you lack wisdom, let him ask of God, that giveth to all men liberally, and upbraideth not; and it shall be given him. But let him ask in faith, nothing wavering. For he that wavereth, is like the wave of the sea driven with the wind and tossed. For let not that man think that he shall receive any thing of the Lord.

James 1:5–8

We must trust God's Word as we would a map. To question it is to make shipwreck of faith, to disregard it is to make shipwreck of ourselves. The old story tells the tale. Just because a farmer boy sees "P. C." in the sky, it doesn't follow that he has received a call to "preach Christ!" More likely it is a heavenly sign that he should "plant corn!" Where many run into difficulty is that they separate subjective faith from objective faith, and thus they command the Lord to do something which He does not intend to do, or they are moved by their emotions rather than their good sense, which leads them into disaster.

Faith is never devoid of reason. In the Gospel of Mark, we have the Lord appearing to a number of men as He walks beside the Sea of Galilee. These were fishermen. He bids them follow Him and He will make them "fishers of men." The men were Peter, Andrew, James, and John, who were to become His disciples. The text says "straightway . . . they followed him" (Mark 1:18,20). These were hardbitten fishermen. Jesus did not have a halo on His head announcing who He was. To the outward eye He was a Jew, as they were. They did not know who He was. Did they just follow

Him, a stranger to them? To do so would have been foolish. The answer is given to us in the fifth chapter of the Gospel of St. Luke. As He is walking by the seaside, the Lord sees the men fishing. He enters one of their boats and would go fishing with them. They tell Him that it is no use. They have fished all night and have caught nothing. To their amazement, He directs them where to fish and they are rewarded with a great catch. They see in this One not merely a stranger or a religious dreamer but one who can really fish. He proves Himself on their wavelength in order that He might bring them to His. He gave them reason to trust Him (*see* Luke 5:1–11). Philip, too, didn't just follow the Lord, as a careless reading of the text might imply (*see* John 1:43,44). Philip was of the same town as Peter and Andrew, and the very mention of this fact would indicate that Philip had learned of the Lord before He said to Philip, "Follow me!" Philip finds Nathanael and tells him of Jesus, and later, Jesus pays Nathanael a great compliment, but he is not impressed. He checks the Living Word, our Lord, against the written Word, the Bible, to see whether Jesus is a false Messiah or the true one. Then he bears witness to the Saviour, "Rabbi, thou art the Son of God; thou art the King of Israel" (John 1:45–49).

Unbelievers, in their scorn, have charged Christians with believing "what ain't so." This may be true of some believers, but if so, it isn't biblical. Neither God nor our Lord pull their rank for us to believe in them just because they are God. Our Lord clearly makes an appeal to reason and experimentation as He addresses the skeptic of His day, "If any man will do his will [God's], he shall know of the doctrine, whether it be of God, or whether I speak of myself" (John 7:17).

The Hindrances to Persistent Thinking

Persistent thinking demands no distractions: it requires a fixed goal, must be certain of its abilities to reach that goal, and cannot allow itself to be dissuaded for any reason from reaching the goal. Its faith in itself and its goal must be unshakable. As far as God is concerned, only the habit of biblical thinking can give us this ability to think persistently until our goal is realized. Unfortunately, however, there are certain things which rob us of a strong faith and weaken our effort in persistent thinking. Among many things we shall note three: trusting in material things instead of God, a pretense of knowing the Lord without really knowing Him, and the habit of doubting His Word. The disciples of Jesus were guilty of these three things. For them, material security was far more important than spiritual security. This is the way of the world. To them He said, ''But seek ye first the Kingdom of God and his righteousness; and all these things shall be added unto you'' (Matthew 6:33). These words are from the Sermon on the Mount. Jesus knew well that trust in material prosperity can be the death of sanctity. In this section of His discourse, the Saviour teaches that earthly wealth has a habit of passing away more quickly than we think. It is subject to inflation and thieves. It leads the heart into greediness and selfishness. It divides the allegiance of man; he cannot serve money and God at the same time. Turning to the things about Him, our Lord points out to His disciples how God takes care of the things of nature—the birds of the air, the lilies of the field. If God is able to take care of them, He can take care of all mankind. ''Wherefore if God so clothe the grass of the field, which today is, and to morrow is cast into the oven, shall he not much more clothe you, O ye of little faith?'' (Matthew 6:30). Many are the promises in the Scriptures which speak of God's care for us. God does know the end from the beginning, and He holds all things in His hands. Thus, as we walk with the Lord in the light of His Word we have every reason to persist in our thinking, to make a reality of our goal. With Paul we can press toward the mark of our high calling.

But in order to do this, we must truly know our Lord. Faith is weakened when Christ is only a theological theory and not a personal friend who can help us in our hour of need. One of the difficulties in trusting Christ is that we have been taught to trust Him as our Saviour for eternal life, but we do not know what that really means since we are involved in temporal life, the things of daily experience. Christ, for all practical purposes, is an idea rather than a living Saviour who is interested in the daily affairs of our personal lives. The disciples are victims of this concept too. On one occasion they are crossing the sea of Galilee when they encounter a storm. Jesus is in the boat, but you would not know it, judging by the conduct of the disciples. In terror of the storm they wake Him. Seeing their distress, He calms the storm. They knew Him. He had chosen them. He had proven Himself to them. But did they really *know* Him? "And he saith unto them, Why are ye fearful, O ye of little faith? Then he arose, and rebuked the winds and the sea; and there was a great calm. But the men marvelled saying, What manner of man is this, that even the winds and the sea obey him!" (Matthew 8:26,27). Though with your lips you profess Him to be the Son of God does your mind still ask, "What manner of man is this?" Is He *only a man* to you? Don't wait until you die to really trust Him; trust Him now for what He is—the eternal Son of God—God in His own right—and let Him calm your fears, let Him guide you through the storms of life, out of the gale into the fair breeze of His blessings.

To do this, however, we cannot doubt His Word. To doubt His Word is to destroy the desire for biblical thinking, so that we never can know its power. Once we become the victim of doubt, we lose the ability to persist against all odds in the reaching of our goal. But if our faith is strong, courage is our portion, and we can press on, making impossible dreams come true. But there are so many things happening to us that would make us doubt God's Word. Peter teaches us a lesson at this point. On this particular occasion, Jesus instructs the disciples to take their boat to the other side of the Sea of Galilee. During the crossing, they encounter one of the many storms for which this sea is known. However, at this crossing the disciples do not panic. Suddenly, they see a figure walking on the water towards them. At first, the disciples think the figure is a ghost and are somewhat troubled. Soon they heard the Lord's voice encouraging them "to be of good cheer." Impulsive Peter does it again! He challenges the identity of his Lord.

And Peter answered him and said, Lord, if it be thou, bid me come unto thee upon the water. And he said, Come. And when Peter was come down out of the ship, he walked on the water, to go to Jesus. But when he saw the wind boisterous, he was afraid; and beginning to sink, he cried, saying, Lord, save me. And immediately Jesus stretched forth his hand, and caught him, and said to him, O thou of little faith, wherefore didst thou doubt? And when they were come into the ship, the wind ceased.

Matthew 14:28–32

Peter's eye was on the wind, not the Saviour. Furthermore, in this instance he made more trouble for himself than was necessary. He should not have challenged the Lord to identify Himself. Then he should not have demanded of the Lord to bid him to walk on the water. Sometimes the Lord lets us have our own will in order to show us that His will is best. But in each of these events which we have recounted the problem was too little faith.

The Demonstration of Persistent Thinking

We now come to the story which led to my conversion. The woman of Canaan gives to us a true demonstration of persistent thinking, thinking which was born of intelligent, unwavering faith in Jesus Christ her Lord. The story is recorded in the fifteenth chapter of St. Matthew. Her daughter was grievously ill and demon possessed. The mother had appealed to the disciples, but they were not able to help her. They considered her a pest and drove her away. She now makes her appeal to Jesus Himself, addressing Him as "Lord, Son of David." He gives her the silent treatment. With this, the disciples order Him to send her away, for they say, "she has been annoying us." He then replies "I am only come to be of help to the children of Israel. I am not sent to Gentiles." This woman was a Gentile (Mark 7:26). The woman takes the snub and the rebuff. The health of her daughter was more important to her than her pride. She cries out, "Lord help me!" In the eyes of the Jews, Gentiles were dogs. They had no Messiah, they were foreigners as far as Israel was concerned, they did not belong to the Covenant. God had promised nothing to those outside the Covenant; they were without God, and they had no hope (*see* Ephesians 2:11,12). Keeping this in mind, we can understand the response of our Lord and the answer of the woman to His Words.

> And he answered and said, It is not meet to take the children's bread, and to cast it to dogs. And she said, Truth, Lord: yet the dogs eat of the crumbs which fall from their masters' table. Then Jesus answered and said unto her, O woman, great is thy faith: be it unto thee even as thou wilt. And her daughter was made whole from that very hour.
>
> Matthew 15:26–28

We can see why the disciples sent her away. They had troubles of their own. But why does the Lord snub her? Why does He rebuff her? Why does He refuse to give her bread? Though the woman does not know it, the Saviour is using her as an object lesson to show what persistent thinking can do when it is born of great faith and love. The disciples are the "in" group. They have been with Him now for a long time. She is an outsider, even a Gentile. But she has a need and she has no doubt in her mind who can meet it. She comes to Jesus with great faith. She is willing to take the silent treatment, she is willing to be rebuffed. She is willing to take a crumb that drops from the children's table, especially since children never forget their dogs. She says in so many words, "Lord, children do not forget their pets, why should You? A crumb from the floor dropped by Your hand is worth more than a whole loaf from any man's table.'' The key is in verse twenty-eight, ''O woman, great is thy faith.'' As God was willing to test Job, knowing he would meet the test, our Lord in the same manner tests the woman, knowing that she would pass with flying colors, in order to show the disciples what unbelievers they were. She had the evidence to believe. She proved her faith and her persistence was rewarded. The disciples were rebuked. It is possible to know about the Lord, biblically, theologically, and doctrinally, without knowing Him really! It is possible to be emotionally moved, to be even ''sent out of this world,'' without really knowing Him down where you daily live. A cyclone experience with the Lord may be just a lot of wind. To breathe quietly the air of the Spirit as you breathe the air of nature is sufficient, as you open the Scriptures and have the Holy Spirit teach you what the Lord can do for you in daily life (*see* John 14:26). Why not do as you often sing? This is the key to persistent thinking which leads to a continual experience in the power of biblical thinking.

> Simply trusting every day,
> Trusting thru' a stormy way;
> Even when my faith is small,
> Trusting Jesus, that is all.
>
> Singing if my way is clear;
> Praying if the path be drear;
> If in danger, for Him call,
> Trusting Jesus, that is all.
>
> Trusting as the moments fly;
> Trusting as the days go by;
> Trusting Him whate'er befall;
> Trusting Jesus, that is all.

EDGAR PAGE STITES

10

The Power
of Surrendered Thinking

IN OUR STUDIES in the power of biblical thinking, we have examined the lives of a number of outstanding men in the Bible in order to see how they have met their personal problems. We now come to the most difficult problem of all, affliction. For our study we return to the life of the apostle Paul, who in his long career mastered the art of biblical thinking, not alone by positive thinking as we saw in chapter three, but now in surrendered thinking, which set him free. Paul demonstrates for us that a physical affliction which could make him a captive and be a liability, when accepted, becomes an asset and sets him free.

People in this world suffer from many physical infirmities. Blindness, deafness, lameness, paralysis, and ill health but to name a few. Such afflictions are not blessings; they are curses. The most difficult thing in life is to tolerate them. I have friends who refuse to tolerate their handicaps. They are continually fighting the thing which they suffer, thus they are a prisoner to it. A very talented individual whom I know wants to be accepted as a man. He refuses to recognize his physical limitation. As a result he will not let himself be trained to cope with his problem. Many have tried to help him, but he has pushed them off. Now he is bitter, his career apparently ruined simply because he has allowed his affliction to be a liability instead of an asset.

The apostle Paul had this choice to make also. He chose to make his affliction an asset. It took some doing. Instead of fighting it, he accepted it. Instead of being a prisoner to his problem, he became free from it. He tells us:

> And lest I should be exalted above measure through the abundance of the revelations, there was given to me a thorn in the flesh, the messenger of Satan to buffet me, lest I should be exalted above measure. For this thing I besought the Lord thrice, that it might depart from me. And he said unto me, My grace is sufficient for thee: for my strength is made perfect in weakness. Most gladly therefore will I rather glory in my infirmities, that the power of Christ may rest upon me. Therefore I take pleasure in infirmities, in reproaches, in necessities, in persecutions, in distresses for Christ's sake: for when I am weak, then am I strong.
>
> 2 Corinthians 12:7–10

What was the problem that was "buffeting" the apostle? The Epistle to the Galatians may give us a clue. At the end of this letter, Paul mentions the large letters in which he has written this note to them (*see* Galatians 6:11). Since it was a letter of rebuke because the Galatians had fallen back into the Law, Paul encourages them to return to a life lived in the spirit of grace. In his argument he points out what great fellowship he had had with them before they became so legalistic and divisive. He reminds them when he was with them that they would do anything for him. He asks "Where is then the blessedness ye spake of? for I bear you record, that, if it had been possible, ye would have plucked out your own eyes, and have given them to me. Am I therefore become your enemy, because I tell you the truth?" (Galatians 4:15,16). Grace is not only sympathetic in word, it is sympathetic in deed as well. So along with his other troubles, Paul may have had an eye problem too.

In seeking a reason for the problem he does not punish himself as to why he has this affliction. He uses his head in thinking quite biblically about it. God had given him a great revelation directly, which he could have used to his own advantage. To do so would have enabled him to boast of his own greatness and abilities. He assumes that his affliction is God's commercial to remind him who is sponsoring his ministry, the God of grace. Paul was not arrogant. Being overwhelmed by God's grace, his humility was not false. Paul had many things of which he could have boasted. He was of the stock of Israel, the tribe of Benjamin, a Hebrew of the Hebrews, a strict Pharisee of the Law. He was a zealot who delighted in persecuting the church. As far as touching the righteousness of the Law, he was blameless. But he renounced these status symbols among his brethren once he had discovered the grace of God. He had only one desire. "That I may know him, and the power of his resurrection, and the fellowship of his sufferings, being made conformable unto his death; If by any means I might attain unto the resurrection of the dead" (Philippians 3:10,11).

Paul refers to his affliction as "the messenger of Satan." Why? You will remember in chapter six of our study, we discussed the life of Job. It may be that Paul had Job in mind, especially the first two chapters of the book, where Satan throws out a challenge to God that only those whom He bribes does God find to have faith in Him. Paul decides, as did Job, to be a witness to God, obeying and loving Him for what He is, not for what one can receive from Him. He also refers to his condition as a "thorn in the flesh." Many times in Scripture this word "thorn" becomes a sign of judgment. As a result of Adam's transgression, nature began to work against man as shown by the thorns that began to grow (*see* Genesis 3:18). In speaking of sinful Israel and God's judgment that was to come to her, Hosea uses this same figure of speech to illustrate the nature of the judgment Israel would experience (*see* Hosea 2:6; 9:6).

In any event, Paul would not argue or complain to God about his condition. He would rest in the Lord and truly wait upon Him. The apostle's problem was not how to avoid his "thorn," but how to accept it.

Accepting the Unacceptable

How did the great apostle go about to accept the unacceptable? How did he turn his liability into an asset? He didn't complain. He turned to God in prayer. He prayed three times that he might be delivered from his thorn in the flesh. Why three times? Doubtless he remembered that his Lord had prayed three times to avoid the cross. To you, devoted reader, my statement "to avoid the cross" is shocking, but hold your fire. For as we turn to this period in the life of our Lord, we may, like Paul, learn a great lesson. It will be a lesson that, when learned, will save us from much agony and hasten us on to the joy of ecstasy as we make our pilgrim journey.

With our Lord, we find ourselves in the Garden of Gethsemane. His disciples are with Him. As He walks farther into the Garden, He takes Peter, James and John with Him. Then He leaves them and goes still farther into the Garden. He is in the shadow of Calvary. Alone, He kneels, He lifts His face to Heaven, He muses, what shall He pray?

> Now is my soul troubled; and what shall I say? Father, save me from this hour: but for this cause came I unto this hour. Father, glorify thy name. Then came there a voice from Heaven, saying, I have both glorified it, and will glorify it again.
>
> John 12:27,28

How could the Lord Jesus Christ, the Son of God raise one question about His not going to the cross? Did he not come to do the Father's will? How could the second person of the Trinity raise any question about the will of the first person of the Trinity? Theologically it is impossible! Sympathetically, with us, it is possible. As our faithful high priest who now intercedes for us, He knew the sorrows and afflictions we would have to bear. He knew the agonies we would experience. So He decided to go to the cross as we would, face suffering and death in order to show us how to do it. This is why we can be victorious over our circumstances instead of being their victims.

Notice what our Lord does in the Garden as recorded by John. He is troubled. He wonders what to do. Should He avoid the cross? But that is why He came into the world, to die. Other men *have to die, He didn't,* for He did not have to collect the wages of sin. But in His death, He would take our death, and in exchange give to us life eternal. As He continues His musing He tells us this is why He came into the world. Then to the Father He prays. He will do the Father's will that lost sinners may be saved.

As we turn to the twenty-sixth chapter of the Gospel of St. Matthew, we have a fully detailed account of our Lord as He prays to His Father in the shadow of Calvary. The quotation which we saw in John's Gospel can be read in twenty-six seconds. Matthew tells us that it took the Lord three hours to pray it. As we examine this passage (26:36–45), we shall see that the Lord prayed three different times. Each time He uses the same words, but there is a negative word, "not," which he moves to a different place each time He prays:

O my Father, if it be possible, let this cup pass from me: nevertheless, *not* as I will, but as thou wilt.

26:39, italics mine

O my Father, if this cup may *not* pass away from me, except I drink it, thy will be done.

26:42, italics mine

O my Father, since this cup will *not* pass away from me, I will drink it.

see 26:44,45

No longer is there an *if,* it is now *since.* The cup will not pass away. Verse forty-five proves it. ''Then cometh he to his disciples, and saith unto them, Sleep on now, and take your rest: behold, the hour is at hand, and the Son of man is betrayed into the hands of sinners.''

Notice how the word *not* shows us how our Lord moves from His will to the will of God. ''If the cup may pass. . . . If the cup may not pass. . . . Since the cup will not pass,'' this is the road of true surrender in biblical thinking. It would have been nothing for the second person of the Godhead to come down and die. He wouldn't have been afraid to die. But like the Father, our Redeemer is not a great computer in the sky, impersonally programmed to do the Father's will, and in the process, treat us as though we were just numbers to be treated indifferently. He came as our great high priest, offering Himself as our Mass, our sacrifice, giving us the first rites of the Church, eternal life, so the last rite would be unnecessary. He died as we cannot, without sin. He died as we might, in agony and fear, in order to be our great high priest who was touched ''with the feeling of our infirmities'' (Hebrews 4:15). And now He is at the Father's throne making intercession for us (Romans 8:34).

Could Paul have heard that ''He [Christ] went away again and prayed the third time saying the same words''? Paul prays three times that he might be delivered from his ''thorn.''

The Joy of Acceptance

Paul differs from us in that he did not tell God the Father how to answer his prayer. Consequently he heard the Father's reply immediately.

> . . . My grace is sufficient for thee: for my strength is made perfect in weakness. Most gladly therefore will I rather glory in my infirmities, that the power of Christ may rest upon me.

Therefore *I take pleasure* in infirmities, in reproaches, in necessities, in persecutions, in distresses for Christ's sake: for when I am weak, then am I strong.

2 Corinthians 12:9,10, italics mine

How could the apostle take pleasure in all these distresses? Was he a morbid soul? Did he enjoy being a martyr? Was he trying to be a hero for God? No! He was practical. He knew how to put God's sovereignty to good use. He used all of these things he mentions as opportunities to show the sufficiency of God's grace. He learned that surrendered thinking can pay great dividends in the coin of heaven. He learned a great biblical fact, to be God's captive is the only way to be free, truly free in an enslaving world.

Paul sets before us two great principles, to accept oneself and to accept the will of God. To fight against either is destructive. To accept both is the key to success in eternal things. If you accept what you are, even at your worst, and accept God as He is, He can make you what you should be in Christ. The trouble with us is that we worry about the pot of clay that we are instead of the treasure we should be (2 Corinthians 4:7). Paul did not believe in God theoretically, as we do; he believed in God realistically, as we should do. When God gave to Paul His answer and not the answer Paul wanted Him to give, Paul, with good sense, considered the matter closed, and began to rejoice even though the problems did not stop, as verse ten of the passage indicates.

We can have this joy too if we learn and practice the art of surrendered thinking. If so, then we shall experience one more phase of the power of biblical thinking.

11

The Power of Sensitive Thinking

SHE WAS A HARLOT—He was a holy man. She was surprised that He asked her for a drink. He was a Jew—she was a Samaritan! He was a *man*—she was a *woman!* She could not understand how He, a Jew, could talk to her, a woman of Samaria. He could understand why she was surprised that He spoke to her, but she didn't know who He was. He was Jesus Christ of Nazareth, the Saviour who came from heaven to save the world from its sin. The record of this encounter is to be found in the fourth chapter of the Gospel of St. John.

Our Lord had just been with one of the great leaders of Israel. Nicodemus had wanted to see Him, so he paid the Saviour a night visit. This teacher of Israel saw in the Man of Galilee not only a great teacher, but because of the miracles He did, a man who truly came from God. Nicodemus knew that no one could do the great works which Jesus did unless God was with Him. We can understand why Nicodemus was amazed at what Jesus was able to do, even though he was mistaken as to who Jesus was. Jesus was not a man come from God, rather, Jesus was God who came to teach and to save.

Without any argument, Jesus says to this religious leader, ''. . . Except a man be born again, he cannot see the kingdom of God'' (John 3:3). The Saviour knew that men did not need religion; they needed salvation, a new life, a life which He brought down from heaven. This is why He said, ''That which is born of the flesh is flesh; and that which is born of the Spirit is spirit. Marvel not that I said unto thee, Ye must be born again'' (John 3:6,7). Our Lord's dealing with Nicodemus is direct, for he was the master teacher of Israel (*see* John 3:10), and as such Nicodemus should have known that the message of salvation was not a new message but was the message of the Old Testament prophets (*see* Ezekiel 36:25–27). Nicodemus, like so many today, did not realize that there is a difference between formal, ritualistic religion and a real, vital faith in God. Had Nicodemus been an authority of the Scriptures instead of tradition, he would not have been surprised at our Lord's teaching (*see* John 3:4,9).

But as we turn to the fourth chapter of John's Gospel, we see that the approach of our Lord to the woman at the well is indirect instead of direct. In this chapter, we have one of the greatest illustrations of sensitive thinking that can be found in the Scriptures. The woman to whom the Lord is speaking has two strikes against her. She is a Samaritan, which would provoke hatred in any Jewish heart. Long ago, the people of Samaria betrayed the Hebrews, who made up the Northern Kingdom, which led to Israel's enslavement. This treachery was not forgotten. Thus we can understand the woman's surprise that Christ speaks to her. She says to Him, ''How is it that thou, being a Jew, askest drink of me, which am a woman of Samaria? for the Jews have no dealings with the Samaritans'' (John 4:9). As a harlot, the woman was a social outcast. She came to the well at the noon hour (*see* 4:6,7). Anyone in his right mind would go to the well for water in the morning or evening when the sun is low and the day is cool. No doubt this social outcast found the tongues of the ''catty'' women much hotter than the noonday sun. Also, the fact that she came alone constantly reminded her of her social position—a harlot to be despised. Daily she came to the well for water, but her thirst was never satisfied. As a harlot, her dalliance with her lovers gave her joy for the moment, but not that true joy that satisfies the human heart.

How does one bring the message of salvation to a harlot? How would we do it? I suppose we would do it in a typical evangelical manner. "What a wretched sinner you are!" we would begin. "Don't you know you should be born again? You are bad enough to go to hell and that is where you are headed if you do not come to Christ!" The poor girl would be frightened by our attack. Hell would be a relief from our condescending smugness. In fact, there is a pretty good chance that we would not even speak to her, lest someone see us and our testimony be compromised because we were seen talking to her. And if she were converted through our witness, we doubtless would put her on parade before our fellow Christians, not as a trophy of God's grace but as an ornament of our efforts in witnessing for Christ.

The Thoughtfulness of Christ

Our Saviour never approached sinners as their critic. He came to them to be their Saviour. In every instance He considered the feelings of those to whom He would speak. Two things in the opening verses of our chapter bring this to our attention. Verse four tells us that He had to go through Samaria to get to Galilee. This necessity was not a matter of geography. He could have crossed over the Jordan, followed the eastern shore northward, and thus He would have bypassed Samaria. By recrossing the Jordan, He would have reached Galilee without difficulty. His necessity was a matter of a soul who needed Him. His sense of timing also shows His consideration for the feelings of this social outcast. He plans to be at the well side at the noon hour. No one else but the woman would be there. He could deal with her case in private, thus avoiding making her an object of disgrace. He even waits until His disciples go into the city to get food before He begins to talk with her (*see* 4:8).

When we witness to people we generally begin with a theological discussion about "sin," "Christ," "salvation," and "God." People rarely know what we are talking about, and in many cases we may not either. The Lord takes a different tack. He makes a request which the woman can understand. He asks for some water to drink (*see* 4:7). This takes her by surprise. As a woman, she is not used to such kindness, especially from the men with whom she associates. Then as a Samaritan, she cannot understand why He, a Jew, will even talk to her (*see* 4:9). The Saviour does not make an issue of her protest. She is there for water and water He will give her.

It is interesting to note that Jesus begins to speak of salvation in a way the woman can understand. She knows about water. It can quench thirst, though not permanently. He begins with what she knows and then moves to what she should know by appealing to an attribute which is common to all women—curiosity. "If thou knewest the gift of God, and who it is that saith to thee, Give me to drink; thou wouldest have asked of him, and he would have given thee living water" (4:10). He focuses her attention not upon God, but upon the water which was the object of her coming to the well. Our Lord keeps her need in mind, and thus does not give her a lesson in theology.

To His declaration she asks an intelligent question: "Sir, thou hast nothing to draw with, and the well is deep: from whence then hast thou that living water?" (4:11). In our witnessing, we should never take sinners for granted. They may know more than meets the eye. We shall see that this harlot is acquainted with the Scriptures. She knows about Jacob, later she will show that she knows about the prophets, and although she is a social outcast, she believes in the coming of the Messiah. This should remind us that when God's Word is planted in the heart of an individual, we should not be discouraged because we do not see immediate spiritual results. It may well be that when we least expect it, the result of our teaching will bear fruit.

Art thou greater than our father Jacob, which gave us the well, and drank thereof himself, and his children, and his cattle? Jesus answered and said unto her, Whosoever drinketh of this water shall thirst again: but whosoever drinketh of the water that I shall give him shall never thirst; but the water that

I shall give him shall be in him a well of water springing up
into everlasting life.

4:12–14

The Lord did not get Himself into a religious argument. The subject
was water, a picture of her need. He now has turned her curiosity
into real interest by pointing out to her that the water of which He
speaks is not H_2O, but spiritual water which can satisfy thirst permanently.

The woman proves that she not only has good sense, but is practical as well. "Sir, give me this water, that I thirst not, neither
come hither to draw" (4:15). Her answer is full of meaning. She
knows that her need is about to be met. To take His water will
quench her thirst forevermore. Too, she will not need to make a
lonely trip to the well in the heat of the day, a reminder to her of
her position as the town's harlot. She mused, "What kind of water
is this that *He* has which will quench my thirst forever?"

The Commendation of Christ

Because of the kindness of Christ to this woman, we might think
that He is never going to deal with her sin. This would be our chief
interest. "Her sin should be judged. She should know what a sinner
she is!" The Saviour differs from us in that He was interested in
saving her rather than putting her down. Well might we take note
of the finesse with which He does it. In fact, He approaches the
question of her sin by the use of a pun. In many languages, the
word "man" and "husband" are translated by the same word. In
answer to her request for the water, He says to her: "Go, call your
man and come here!" The woman answered and said, "I have no
man!" Jesus does not condemn her for lying. He will commend her
for telling the truth. "Well have you said, 'I have no man.' You
have had five men, and the one that you now have is not your man.
Indeed you have spoken the truth" (*see* 4:16–18).

Had a harlot told us that she had lived with five men and now she is living with a sixth man, we would have raised our hands in holy horror. We would have condemned her without mercy. In fact, we would have stopped our witness lest we be polluted by her presence. The Lord takes the occasion to commend her for telling the truth. And hearing His commendation, she comes to the conclusion that He must be a prophet. This is one more evidence of the religious training she must have had in her youth. Not only did she know about Jacob and the well, she also knew the purpose of a prophet as well.

This realization on her part that she is speaking to a prophet leads her into a discussion of some Old Testament history with Him. She raises the question where should one worship.

> Our Fathers worshipped in this mountain; and ye say, that in Jerusalem is the place where men ought to worship. Jesus said unto her, Woman, believe me, the hour cometh, when ye shall neither in this mountain, nor yet at Jerusalem, worship the Father. Ye worship ye know not what: we know what we worship: for salvation is of the Jews. But the hour cometh, and now is, when the true worshippers shall worship the Father in spirit and in truth: for the Father seeketh such to worship him. God is a Spirit, and they that worship him must worship him in spirit and in truth.
>
> 4:20–24

Though men are sinners, they may be religious too. The woman tries to involve our Lord in a religious argument, as the text shows. Where should one really worship? Her tradition dictates that worship should be at this mountain site where her fathers worshiped. The Saviour says that Jerusalem is the place to worship. Both were right. The woman knew her religious history. Indeed, Jacob did worship at that spot (*see* Genesis 33:20). Furthermore, the mountains to which she referred had been very important in Israel's early history (*see* Deuteronomy 11:29). Here God had given Israel a review of the Law before they entered the Land of Canaan. He had told His people that if they would obey Him there would be blessing for them. If they disobeyed Him, His curse would be their portion. So that they would not forget the warning, Moses instructed Joshua to place the symbol of the blessing of Mount Gerizim and the symbol of the curse on Mount Ebal (*see* Deuteronomy 11:27–32). As Israel entered the Land of Promise under the leadership of Joshua, this command of Moses was carried out (*see* Joshua 8:30–35). This reference to Israel's history by the woman leaves no doubt of her previous religious training.

When Israel became settled in the Promised Land, Jerusalem became the permanent place of worship. Our Lord gives us a good example as to how to avoid nonessentials when dealing with a soul about salvation. In so many words He says, "Why worry about where you are to worship. The fact is you are still thirsty. Furthermore, God is not interested in the geographical place of worship. Do you worship Him with your heart in righteousness and truth?" Formal religion has its place if it is not devoid of a living faith in the Saviour. Israel had a great formal religion, but their hearts were not in it (*see* Deuteronomy 5:29).

This woman again shows that she is not only religious, but practical as well. She does not argue with the Lord. She replies, "I know that Messias cometh, which is called Christ: when he is come he will tell us all things. Jesus saith unto her, I that speak unto thee am he" (John 4:25,26). This woman knows that the Messiah will come someday. She knows what He is to do when He comes. Jesus declares Himself to be the Messiah. She does not argue with Him, because He has proven to her that He is truly the Messiah who is to come. He tells her—gently to be sure—that she is a harlot. He tells her she needs water that will cause her never to thirst again. He reveals to her the secret of true worship—to worship God in Spirit and in truth (*see* 4:23,24). She believes Him and becomes a missionary.

The Harlot Becomes a Missionary

In a most unorthodox manner, the harlot becomes a missionary and brings many to Christ before the astonished eyes of the disciples. While they are arguing theology, she is winning souls. The only thing wrong about what she does is that she does not do it as we would have her do it.

First, she does not confess she is a harlot, nor does she declare her faith in Christ by telling Him she is born again. Further, she does not get the Lord's permission to see if she is worthy to proclaim the message of salvation. She does not even wait to see if the Lord will tell her that her background might be a liability in Christian service. What she does may be unorthodox from our point of view, but I have no doubt the Lord was delighted in what she did do.

It is interesting to note that the disciples are thorough-going evangelicals in that they question what they see—our Lord talking to a harlot.

And upon this [the conversation with the woman] came his disciples, and marvelled that he talked with the woman; yet no man said, What seekest thou? or, Why talkest thou with her? The woman then left her waterpot, and went her way into the city, and saith to the men, Come, see a man, which told me all things that ever I did; is not this the Christ?

4:27–29

As we are, the disciples are critics instead of missionaries. The disciples, like good "holy Joes," take out in thinking what they dare not to ask Him. They trust their suspicions instead of His integrity. No wonder He had to say to them on many occasion "O ye of little faith."

It is true the woman never confesses to being born again, rather she confesses it in action, not in words. *She leaves her waterpot!*

What a confession of faith. No longer does she need it. She finds
the spring of living water bubbling in her heart. What else can she
do but tell others of this living water? Whom better can she tell but
the men whom she knows only too well? Doubtless the change in
the woman is so evident that they believe her testimony. They
follow her to the seventh man—the man from heaven, Christ Jesus.

Read the record:

> Come, see a man, which told me all things that ever I did:
> is not this the Christ? Then they went out of the city, and
> came unto him. . . . And many of the Samaritans of that city
> believed on him for the saying of the woman, which testified,
> He told me all that ever I did. So when the Samaritans were
> come unto him, they besought him that he would tarry with
> them: and he abode there two days. And many more believed
> because of his own word; And said unto the woman, Now we
> believe not because of thy saying: for we have heard him our-
> selves, and know that this is indeed the Christ, the Saviour of
> the world.
>
> 4:29,30,39–42

The joy of the Lord is her strength. She goes to her companions in
sin, brings them to Christ, and they become her companions in
sainthood. Their first desire is to have Christ stay with them so that
they can hear His Word. As a result, many more confess their faith
in Him. Two things we must observe about the woman which make
her a great missionary: She believes the Lord to be the Messiah; she
drops her waterpot at His feet. Thus unencumbered, she proclaims
the message "Come, see a man. . . ." One never needs to be
ashamed of forgiven sin.

The woman learns one great lesson from her Saviour which
many of us have yet to learn. She sees that the Saviour came to
save her, not to condemn her (*see* John 3:16,17), and with that

spirit she goes to the men who merit judgment, and offers them salvation. Though the Lord knows what she is, He lets her tell Him.
He approaches her in tenderness and mercy. She already knows
what she deserves. Her waterpot and her lonely trek daily to the
well speak volumes to her. Receiving the grace of God from His
lips of mercy, she does not turn it to judgment when speaking to
her fellows. Had it been written, the Samaritans might have sung:

> In tenderness He sought me,
> Weary, and sick with sin.
> And on His shoulders brought me
> Back to His fold again;
> While angels in His presence sang,
> Until the courts of heaven rang.
>
> He washed the bleeding sin wounds
> And poured in oil and wine;
> He whispered, to assure me,
> "I've found thee, thou art Mine."
> I never heard a sweeter voice—
> It made my aching heart rejoice:
>
> O the love that sought me!
> O the blood that bought me!
> O the grace that brought me to the fold!
> Wondrous grace that brought me to the fold.

W. SPENCER WALTON

Thinking of Others' Feelings

Do you consider the feeling of others, especially if they differ
from yours? Even though they were with their Lord for about three
years, the disciples could never forget themselves and their self-
righteousness. They would rather argue and criticize over how a
thing should be done, thus they never got anything done. This is

evident from the rebuke the Lord gives to them as the men to whom the woman witnessed are coming out of the city. Pointing to the on-coming crowd, the Saviour says to His own, "Say not ye, There are yet four months, and then cometh harvest? behold, I say unto you, Lift up your eyes, and look on the fields; for they are white already to harvest" (4:35). They too have a waterpot which they have yet to drop at the feet of the Saviour. They expect Him to be the Messiah—not the One who will tell them all things. They expect Him to be the One who will rule over the earth, and that they will reign with Him. Instead they face the future with a Saviour who will wear a crown of thorns, and they will be scattered abroad to be persecuted and to suffer. When thinking of one's own interests, it is difficult to be aware of the interests of others.

May we examine our relationship to Jesus Christ to see what we hope to gain from it. Do we believe in Christ for what we can get out of Him, or do we believe Him for what we can do for Him by witnessing to others of Him? Do we approach the lost with the tender spirit of His grace, so we may demonstrate that we possess for ourselves the living water for which the world thirsts? May we be sensitive to the feeling of others, and may their confidence in us lead them to the Saviour.

12

The Mind of Christ

WE HAVE NOTED the importance of godly thinking in our first chapter. Following this, we have seen the positive thinking of Paul, the negative thinking of Moses, the transformed thinking of Jeremiah, the faithful thinking of Job, and the arrogant thinking of Peter. We examined the persistent thinking of the woman of Canaan, which was born of a strong faith. We returned to Paul as an illustration of surrendered thinking made necessary through a troublesome physical problem. In this chapter, we shall examine the mind of Christ Himself. It is important that we do so, for as Christians who bear His name, we should know how He thought in order for us to "be conformed to his image" (*see* Romans 8:29).

In the second chapter of the Philippian Epistle, the Apostle Paul gives us a clear presentation of the mind of Christ.

> Let this mind be in you, which was also in Christ Jesus: Who, being in the form of God, thought it not robbery to be equal with God. But made himself of no reputation, and took upon him the form of a servant, and was made in the likeness of men. And being found in fashion as a man, he humbled himself, and became obedient unto death, even the death of the cross.
>
> Philippians 2:5–8

To the theologian, this passage lends itself to a discussion between the divine and human natures of Christ, as seen in the philosophical belief of those who are interested, as to how far our Divine Lord "humbled" [emptied] Himself. We shall not enter this *kenotic* discussion, for we are interested in the practical aspects of the passage. Since I am basically addressing you my readers, as God's sheep, at another time we can go into a discussion of the problem when addressing God's giraffes.

"Let this mind be in you, which was also in Christ Jesus." Here Paul admonishes us to have the mind of Christ. In order to do so, we must know what that mind is. Following his exhortation, the apostle gives us seven characteristics which our Lord demonstrated while on earth which make clear to us how His mind worked when He was among us.

In the first place, the Saviour knew who He was. He was as much God as God the Father and God the Holy Spirit. "Who, being in the form of God, thought it not robbery to be equal with God." He was with God at the creation. "In the beginning was the Word, and the Word was with God, and the Word was God. The same was in the beginning with God. All things were made by him; and without him was not anything made that was made. . . . And the Word was made flesh, and dwelt among us. . . (John 1:1–3,14). Later, in His incarnation, He would say, "I and my Father are one" (John 10:30). This oneness is that of essence, not of person. Their attributes were in common, their purposes were the same, and whatever was done they did together, each sharing a phase of creation and redemption. Thus, Jesus did not rob God of anything when He declared Himself to be God. He knew who He was.

"He made himself of no reputation." When our Lord came to earth, though He was the second person of the Trinity, He came as the Son of Man to be one of us. He did not come to pull His rank, to do so would have been rank. "The Word was made flesh . . . and we beheld his glory . . . full of grace and truth" (John 1:14). Christmas cards notwithstanding, He did not have a halo on His head. To the eye of men, Jesus was just another Jew. He was born, not within the families of the rich, but of the poor. When Mary,

His mother, went to offer the sacrifice of purification she did not have the required sacrifice of the wealthy; she offered the sacrifice of those born to poverty (*see* Luke 2:24). And in a point of His ministry, the Lord of Heaven and Earth would say, ". . . The foxes have holes, the birds of the air have nests; but the Son of man hath not where to lay his head" (Matthew 8:20). Well is He named Emmanuel (*see* Matthew 1:23), for He is *with us* as God in more ways than one.

"He took upon him the form of a servant." This was His commission. He came to serve God the Father, not in the role of Deity, but in the role of humanity; not as the Lord, but as the ministering servant. Of Himself He said, "For even the Son of man came not to be ministered unto, but to minister, and to give his life a ransom for many" (Mark 10:45). The term "ransom" takes us back to the Old Testament, to the Day of Atonement, "Yom Kippur," where the offering for sins was made by the priests on behalf of Israel. Christ came to minister not only in life, but in death as well. Thus the Good Shepherd speaks. "I am the good shepherd, and know my sheep, and am known of mine. As the Father knoweth me, even so I know the Father: and I lay down my life for the sheep" (John 10:14,15). And throughout His earthly ministry, our Lord maintained this spirit of humble service. He could be firm when necessary, and angry when the wickedness of men called it forth, but He was gentle and thoughtful toward the poor and needy.

"He was made in the likeness of men." Why could not Christ, as God, have gone to the cross without becoming man? Why did not the Father invent some other way to atone for our sins apart from the incarnation? God was not merely interested in the act of redemption for sin. This was necessary to meet the demands of His holiness and justice. His love demanded that He care for us. Christ became one of us to feel with us, to sympathize with us, to enable us to see in Him One who cares. As the writer to the Hebrews expressed it, "For we have not an high priest which cannot be touched with the feeling of our infirmities; but was in all points tempted like as we are, yet without sin. Let us therefore come boldly unto the throne of grace, that we may obtain mercy, and find grace to help in time of need'' (Hebrews 4:15,16). And because of this we can sing:

> Come, ye disconsolate, where'er ye languish—
> Come to the mercy-seat, fervently kneel;
> Here bring your wounded hearts, here tell your anguish:
> Earth has no sorrow that heav'n cannot heal.
>
> Joy of the desolate, light of the straying,
> Hope of the penitent, fadeless and pure!
> Here speaks the Comforter, tenderly saying,
> ''Earth has no sorrow that heav'n cannot cure.''
>
> Here see the Bread of Life, see waters flowing
> Forth from the throne of God, pure from above;
> Come to the feast of love—come ever knowing,
> Earth has no sorrow but heaven can remove.

THOMAS MOORE

THOMAS HASTINGS

Not only would He sympathize with us, but He at the same time became a man that He might rob us of the fear of death. For the world, death is a funeral, a grave, and fear of the unknown. Christ came to rob us of this fear (*see* Hebrews 2:14,15). Our hope in Him enables us to see what men call *death* to be but the entrance into eternal life, whereby we see by sight the One who for many years we have taken by faith. As Paul so beautifully puts it, death is just a departure, for to be absent from the body is to be at home with the Lord (*see* 2 Corinthians 5:8).

''And being found in the fashion as a man, he humbled himself.'' Among theologians, the word *humbled* has caused much discussion. How did He *humble* or *empty* Himself they ask? We shall not enter the discussion of *kenosis* (from the Greek word for "humbled") here. From a practical viewpoint, what the Lord really did was to move from the wavelength of His deity to operate on the wavelength of our humanity. Though He was still God, He set aside the prerogatives of His deity and limited Himself to the prerogatives of sinless humanity. Thus becoming one with us in poverty (*see* 2 Corinthians 8:9), as an example of obedience to do the Father's will (*see* John 5:30), He takes upon Himself the wrath which was meant for us at Calvary.

We read that: "He became obedient." He listened to the Father's will and did it. The word *obedient* in the Greek text gives the idea of hearing in the sense of getting under what you are listening to and doing something about it. The will of the Father was that Christ should come and die that He might be the Saviour of sinners. This is what the Lord agreed to do. This is why He is the delight to the Father and is loved by Him (*see* John 10:17,18). The Lord Jesus Christ was not forced by the Father to be the world's Saviour. Christ's coming into the world was the result of a committee in heaven. The Father had a problem: He would save us by His love and grace, but to do so would violate His justice. He had declared that the soul that sins shall die. Animal sacrifices could never take away sin. Jesus agreed to die that sinners might be saved justly as well as graciously (*see* Hebrews 10:5–7). Hebrews ten records the farewell words to the father as Christ leaves heaven for earth.

"He was obedient unto death, even the death of the cross." Christ came to save us from eternal death, eternal separation from God, which was caused by our sin and rebellion against God. There is only one great sin which the Scripture recognizes, out of which all the other sins of men are but a by-product. The sin which the Bible recognizes is to be less perfect than God (Romans 3:23). Furthermore, men are religious. They play "hide and seek" with God. But God knows who is "it." It isn't He! (Romans 3:10–12). Everyone will account for his conduct, for he is answerable to God for it (Romans 3:19,20). Thus we can only please God insofar as we are seen by Him through the merits of our Saviour.

Not the labors of my hands
Can fulfill thy law's demands;
Could my zeal no respite know,
Could my tears for ever flow,
All for sin could not atone;
Thou must save, and thou alone.

Nothing in my hand I bring:
Simply to thy cross I cling;
Naked, come to thee for dress;
Helpless, look to thee for grace:
Foul, I to the fountain fly;
Wash me, Savior, or I die!

AUGUSTUS M. TOPLADY

To summarize what we have studied, there are seven great characteristics which make up the mind of our Saviour, as seen in Philippians two: His identification, He knew Who He was; no reputation, He did not pull His rank; His commission, He came into the world as the servant of the Father; His position, He became a man to be one with us; His attitude, He demonstrated true humility; His obedience, He came to do the Father's will; His goal, He came to die on Calvary's cross for us and the whole world of sinners.

How can this mind of Christ be in us?

Christ's Mind in Us

Is it possible for us to have the mind of Christ? Must we go to Jerusalem, outside a city wall and die on a cross? What does it really mean to have the mind of Christ? In the sixth chapter of Romans, at verse four, we have the key to the answer to the question. "Therefore we are buried with him by baptism into death: that like as Christ was raised up from the dead by the glory of the Father, even so we also *should walk in newness of life*" (Romans

6:4, italics mine). Christ did the dying, we are to do the living. How can we put the characteristics of Christ's mind into our thinking? Let us transpose the passage of our study and see if we can make a practical, spiritual application of its truth.

We shall let this mind, which was also in Christ Jesus be in us. For, being in the form of sinful men, we think it not robbery to be equal with sinful men. But we make ourselves of no reputation, having taken upon ourselves the form of a servant, since we have been made into the likeness of our Lord. And having been made in the likeness of our Lord, we humble ourselves, and become obedient unto life, even the life of our risen Lord.

As members of Adam's sinful race, we are sinful like the rest of mankind. Although we have been redeemed, the seeds of sin are still within us (*see* John 1:8–10). When we show fits of anger, flashes of pride, times of worry, we are showing the conduct of the old nature which spoils the spiritual fruit of the new nature. We are not robbing our unsaved friends of anything. We share their nature and we show it when we are off duty as saints.

Our Lord made Himself of no reputation, neither should we. As children of God we should never pull our rank as sinners. When I was a pastor in a church in the eastern part of our country, I visited a certain plant in order to do some business with one of the officials. When we were finished, I told the man I was visiting that I understood one of my church members, a church officer, worked in his plant. As I mentioned his name, the official of the firm offered to take me down to my friend's department. As we left the elevator and began to walk down the hall toward the office, I heard a verbal fight going on. The language used was not to be found in the Bible. Nearing the office door, I recognized the voice of the one using the profanity. It was my church official, a born again one, a good Bible student, who on occasion had the habit of advising the Trinity. We stood outside the door for a moment. "Do me a favor," I said, "let us go away. I do not want to embarrass John. Don't tell him I was here!"

A month later, we had a business meeting of the officials of my church. John was in the group. We were seeking ways to advance the witness of our congregation in the neighborhood and each man present gave his idea as to how it might be done. The chairman then asked me what I thought. Having a good memory and a sense of the dramatic, I dramatized what I had heard that day behind that office door. We were all agreed that the way was novel, but hardly fitting for witnessing to our neighbors about Christ.

After the meeting, I went next-door to the parsonage. As the family was about to sit down for some coffee and pie in the kitchen, a knock was heard. The door opened and there was John. I invited him to have some pie with us. After the grace was said and we began eating, he asked, "Pastor, were you in our plant about a month ago?" "Why do you ask?" I wanted to know. "Pastor, I heard your drama tonight. I know where you got the script. I am so ashamed. I don't know what to think or say." I explained to him how I liked to visit our men at work, which he knew. I told John I had business to transact in one of the other departments of his firm. I told one of his colleagues how proud I was of him and he offered to bring me down to his office. I heard the fighting behind the door. "I stole away so you wouldn't be embarrassed. I was there for only a few minutes. John, as I stood by the door I wondered how often the Holy Spirit who indwells your heart has to listen as you quarrel."

I did not wait for an answer. We spoke of other things. I knew the Holy Spirit would show him that it is shameful when a Christian pulls his sinful rank in any given situation. One thoughtless official saw the point, and through his personal revival a whole church received great revival without one invitation. When we present our bodies to Christ as living sacrifices, we are never in danger of acting like a saint off duty from a life of godliness.

Like our Lord, we too become servants of the heavenly Father. With Him we share the Father's glory in order that we may be a blessing to those with whom we associate. Paul spoke of himself as a bondslave of Christ. As a missionary throughout the world of his day Paul gave everything he had: the ability of his mind, the strength of his body, and the steadfastness of his will, to the proclamation of the Gospel. The reason he could do this was because he had no mental reservations concerning the message he proclaimed (*see* Romans 1:1–17). In turn, Paul exhorts all the followers of the Lord Jesus Christ to do the same (*see* Romans 12:1,2).

As Jesus came from heaven to be the Son of man, He did so that through salvation, we might become the sons of God. We read in the Gospel of St. John, "But as many as received him, to them gave he power to become the sons of God, even to them that believe on his name" (John 1:12). The important verb in this verse is "become." We are to become what we are. Too often many receive Christ as their Saviour and assume by that acceptance that now they are Christians. They are in name and in fact, but it is necessary to make that fact a vital reality. When a soldier enlists in the army, a soldier he is, but not in terms of the battlefield. He has to become what he is officially. As our Lord lived on our level as the Son of man, we must learn to live on His level as a son of God. This is accomplished through our growth in grace as we master the art of biblical thinking. The Holy Spirit then can take God's Word and cause it to live in our hearts, which in a wonderful way, gives new direction to our conduct. God's goal for us is that we are to become Xerox copies of the Saviour (*see* Romans 8:29).

Above, as we studied the humility of Christ, we noted that He came down to our level to be one with us. For some reason, the general notion of humility which we hold seems to say that we are to be absolutely nothing. The more we demean ourselves, the more spiritual we think we are. This is not the teaching of the text. True humility demands that we be something, not nothing. We must remember that our new "I" has risen with Christ and as a new

"I," we are to walk in the power of our risen Lord. We must do the walking. Thus, humility for us is to rise to His level that we may live as the sons of God among the sons of men. Paul makes this very clear, "I therefore, the prisoner of the Lord, beseech you that ye *walk worthy* of the vocation wherewith ye are called" (Ephesians 4:1, italics mine). I know that we want the Lord to have all the credit, but He gets more credit when we are something. He gets no credit when we are nothing. He has given us everything we need to live for Him, but we must use these provisions He has given.

Christ was obedient; He was careful to do the Father's will. We are to be obedient also. In the Bible we find the directions as to how we can please our Divine Lord and our heavenly Father. The words which our Lord addressed to the disciples, apply to us today.

> Come unto me, all ye that labour and are heavy laden, and I will give you rest. Take my yoke upon you, and learn of me: for I am meek and lowly in heart: and ye shall find rest unto your souls. For my yoke is easy, and my burden is light.
>
> Matthew 11:28–30

As we master the Word of God we "learn of Him." He is able to instruct us, correct us, direct us, and efficiently equip us to become true men and women of God (*see* 2 Timothy 3:16,17).

He was obedient unto death, even the death of the cross. Our Saviour meets us at the cross. He takes our death, and we receive His life. Now we are to be "obedient unto life, even the life of our risen Lord." As we, through the Scriptures, identify ourselves with Him, as we learn what He would have us do, *as we do it,* then the mind of Christ is operating in us and our lives take on that heavenly character which shows the sons of men that we are truly sons of God. Then Paul's admonition has been answered. "Let this mind

be in you which was also in Christ Jesus.'' As we sing many times,
may we live always:

> Not a burden we bear, Not a sorrow we share,
> But our toil He doth richly repay;
> Not a grief nor a loss, Not a frown nor a cross,
> But is blest if we trust and obey.

> But we never can prove The delights of His love,
> Until all on the altar we lay,
> For the favor He shows And the joy He bestows,
> Are for them who will trust and obey.

> When we walk with the Lord In the light of His Word,
> What a glory He sheds on our way!
> While we do His good will, He abides with us still,
> And with all who will trust and obey.

JOHN H. SAMMIS

13

The Power of Personal Thinking

SO FAR IN OUR STUDY, we have examined some of the great characters in the Scriptures as to how they mastered the art of biblical
thinking, and how their lives were changed by it. In our last chapter, we saw the mind of our Lord in action in order to demonstrate
how biblical thinking can be put into practice. In the same chapter
we suggested how we might have Christ's mind operating in us
today. As readers, you may be asking yourselves, "How does the
author of this book master the art of biblical thinking? What power
has he received from it?" I have experimented with it and have not
found it wanting. I have found real power in personal biblical
thinking.

In the summer of 1934, I was graduated from the Moody
Bible Institute, in Chicago, Illinois. On the day before gradua-
tion, I sat in the office of the late Dr. P. B. Fitzwater, Professor of Theology, and we had our farewell talk. During our conversation he said, "Ralph, you have the gift of gab, which is
good. Only remember this, God has only promised to bless His
Word, not yours. In your preaching and teaching make God's Word
prominent in what you say. Further, you have a good mind. I have
no doubt that you will go on to college and the university for further study. You may find subjects in these schools far more exciting
than those taught here at Moody. You may even find professors
who are more brilliant and approachable than some of us. They will
become your friends. If you have any love and regard for me, as I
believe you do, promise me you will do one thing: Between your

favorite study, and your favorite professor, *keep the Book* (the Bible)!'' Since that conversation with Dr. Fitzwater, I have been to a number of schools and universities. I did discover subjects which were far more interesting and challenging than those which I studied at Moody. I greatly admired some of my university professors for their brilliance and their knowledge in their field of philosophy. But from the day I heard Dr. Fitzwater say, ''Keep the Book,'' I have faithfully carried out his words and fulfilled the promise I made to him. I have studied the thoughts of the greatest of men always in the light of the Scriptures.

No doubt Dr. Fitzwater had in mind the words of God through Solomon, ''Trust in the Lord with all thine heart; and lean not unto thine own understanding. In all thy ways acknowledge him, and he shall direct thy paths'' (Proverbs 3:5,6).

In line with the promise I made to my beloved professor, I chose as my life verse the words which God gave to Joshua upon the death of Moses. Joshua had the task of leading Israel into the Promised Land. It was a great undertaking. Said God to Joshua:

This book of the law shall not depart out of thy mouth; but thou shalt meditate therein day and night, that thou mayest observe to do according to all that is written therein: for then thou shalt make thy way prosperous, and then thou shalt have good success. Have not I commanded thee? Be strong and of a good courage; be not afraid, neither be thou dismayed: for the LORD thy God is with thee whithersoever thou goest.

Joshua 1:8,9

Thus I started my journey into the world of biblical thinking. Being of a rational turn of mind, I wanted to know the *why* of every *what* the Bible presented. When God gave a command, I wanted to know the reason for it. When a thing was forbidden I wanted to know *why*. This was very important to me since I worked in a world of unbelievers. They saw I did things which they did not do, and in turn, they did things which I didn't. They would want to know the reason for the differences in our mode of living. At first I could offer no intelligent answer. I stood like a dunce, not knowing what to say. Tiring of my ignorance, I searched the Scriptures for answers to questions as to why, as believers, we had a given mode of conduct by which we should live. The answers were in the Bible in abundance. Mastering them, I had an answer to give my fellows. No longer was I embarrassed; they were, because the answers from the Bible made such good sense. I began to relish the truth from Peter's epistle that we can give a reason for the hope that is within us (*see* 1 Peter 3:15).

Having been saved at a Bible conference where God's Word was taught, and becoming a member of a church which was known for its Bible teaching, I was brought up in a spiritual atmosphere where it was the natural thing for a Christian to study the Scriptures in order to grow in grace (*see* 1 Peter 2:2,3). My spiritual mentors advised me to have daily devotions, which I found soon to be a waste of time. I am sure the fault was not with the devotions; it was my method. I used to read the Scriptures aimlessly, pray ritually, and when I was finished, I wondered what I had done. I have no doubt that God, though being omniscient, also had trouble figuring out what I was doing. I came to the conclusion I had to change my method if devotional time was to become valuable.

I discovered that if I disciplined myself to read the Bible through in a year, I could do it by reading three chapters on a week day and five on Sunday. Just to read the Scriptures through in a year, really proves nothing. So I thought I ought to take a subject and read the Bible through in the light of it. I began with the doctrine of God, then Christ, then the Holy Spirit. I also studied the doctrine of man. By the time I was through, I not only had what the Scriptures taught on these subjects, I saw how each book progressively unfolded each truth.

Having chosen a given subject, I would read my assigned

number of chapters for each day. When I came to a passage which dealt with the subject, I would record the reference in a notebook, but would continue reading my assigned chapters. Later, at a time apart from my devotion time, I would make an analysis of the passage, learning the *what* and the *why* of it. After doing this for a number of years, I discovered that I was memorizing the Bible as well as reading it.

Not only did I choose doctrinal subjects for my devotional studies, but practical problems as well. I have only 10 percent of normal vision. With Job I wondered, "Why should this be?" One year I took various afflictions as my theme. When I finished I had the assurance that God could use me to His glory, and with Paul I knew God's strength would perfect my weakness. If we are willing to glorify God, He will undertake it for us. Many times He doesn't when we are not willing.

Graduating from an eastern college, I desired to go to a certain seminary. I was advised that I would not be acceptable to that denomination because of my handicap, so there was no use attempting to enter this particular seminary. It was a terrific blow to me at the time, for the moment. However, I knew that if I was willing to glorify God in the gutter, somehow He would work things out and bring me to the curb. The Scripture carried me over the bridge of depression. God's sovereignty saved me from agony. Why be wretched? I couldn't do anything about it. It was God's problem and He would work it out (*see* Philippians 2:12–16). The fact that I have written what you are reading is a witness to God's faithfulness. Sometimes we have to begin glorifying God in left field, or behind the eight ball, or at least where we do not wish to do it.

There was a time in my life when I thought of marriage. All my friends were marrying wonderful girls and I thought, "Why shouldn't I?" I mused, "I don't see well. What right do I have to ask a girl to marry me? How can she know what it will be like to live with a person of limited vision? There are many things she will have to do for herself which a man who could see well would do for her.'' I was somewhat fearful at this point. However, when one memorizes the Scripture the Holy Spirit has something to bring to that person's remembrance. He reminded me that John wrote, ''There is no fear in love; but perfect love casteth out fear: because fear hath torment. He that feareth is not made perfect in love. We love him, because he first loved us'' (1 John 4:18,19). In the light of this verse I determined not to be afraid of my romantic future. I would love Him and let Him direct my path (*see* Psalms 32:8).

A young lady I liked, who later became my wife, was an employee of the Evangelical Foundation, publisher of *Eternity Magazine,* for whom we both worked. At a banquet she was sitting at my side. There were no waitresses to serve us. Each person had been given a number, mine was four, her's was five. When it came for me to do the duty of four, I saw she had changed the numbers. Upon asking her for the reason, Nan said, ''Number four is liquid, number five is solid. I thought you could manage the solid rather than carrying and pouring the coffee.'' I thought, ''That girl has insight. I must look into this more closely.'' On our first date, we were walking through a park. A pigeon got fresh. Nan took our her little handkerchief and daubed the bird's freshness away. Rising to the occasion, she said, ''Let us be thankful elephants don't fly!'' I was convinced she would be the girl for me. With such insight and understanding, God was bringing someone into my life who could cope with a person with limited vision. For twenty-four years she has done it beautifully.

There is power in biblical thinking when one needs to face an operation and when the loss of all vision is possible. For eight years I put off the operation because I did not want to lose what vision I had. I worked among the visually handicapped. I had taken many to hospitals for operations and they were very successful operations indeed. But I thought, ''Why shouldn't I be the one to keep the law of averages going?'' Then I did a very foolish thing. One night, in the city of Philadelphia, at one of its churches, I preached on the subject ''God's Grace is Sufficient for Every Situation!'' I was preaching with great liberty. Suddenly the Holy Spirit brought to my mind that I was lying to the people. I suggested that He could at least wait until tomorrow to tell me. I did not want Him to interrupt a good sermon. He insisted, however, and told me that at least I should be honest with the people. "Why don't you tell them that the grace of God is sufficient for everyone but you?" He asked. "But the Bible says it is sufficient for everyone," I replied. "That is correct," He responded, "but you know it is not true for you. You have not been willing to trust the Lord for your eye operation." I knew what He meant. I was not telling the people the truth. I was so impressed by this that I interrupted the sermon I was preaching to the people and told them what the Holy Spirit was telling me. It is dangerous to memorize the Scriptures, for the Holy Spirit brings it to our minds when we wish He would not. The congregation that night got two sermons for one offering.

The next day, I called the eye surgeon to make arrangements for the operation. He had me come down to his office to tell him why I had changed my mind. "What were the psychological factors," he wanted to know, "that made you change your mind?" I told him it was not a matter of psychology. It was the sin of unbelief. I really did not believe that God could care for me if the operation went wrong. In fact, I may have believed that God could care for me if I had become totally blind. I just did not want the inconvenience. He was impressed to see my lack of fear and my interpretation of my change of heart, as I witnessed to my Christian faith and how God, through His Word, can trap us when it pleases Him. There is no greater joy than to be trapped for the glory of God.

Obey and Save a Prayer

In the experiences I have related one can see that in each God's Word played an important part. Obedience to His Word is the key to the power of biblical thinking. God can never bless us if we do not obey Him. Prayer cannot be a substitute for obedience. Early in my Christian experience, I learned not only the importance of trusting God, I learned something which was more important to me. *Can God trust me?* Two passages of Scripture influenced me greatly. "If ye abide in me, and my words abide in you, ye shall ask what ye will, and it shall be done unto you" (John 15:7). "My little children, let us not love in word, neither in tongue; but in deed and in truth. And whatsoever we ask, we receive of him, because we keep his commandments, and do those things that are pleasing in his sight" (1 John 3:18,22).

Obedience goes a long way with God. I believe we can save ourselves a great number of prayer meetings if we take Him at His Word and do what He tells us.

Would you know the power of biblical thinking? Let us suppose gossip is your favorite indoor sport. At church you heard a wonderful piece of it, and the person who should have heard it wasn't there. You want to be the first to tell her. You rush home from church, and as soon as you are in the house you call your friend. To your consternation, the line is busy. You know that someone is calling her first. However, you try again and the line is clear. Suddenly, to his surprise, your husband sees you dropping the receiver to its cradle. "Why aren't you completing the call?" "I just remembered," replies the wife. "I had my devotions this morning and the Holy Spirit is bringing it to my remembrance. 'Let the words of my mouth, and the meditation of my heart, be acceptable in thy sight, O LORD, *my strength,* and my redeemer' (Psalms 19:14, italics mine). He says I have the strength and my words must be acceptable in His sight." What a wonderful way not to gossip. What a wonderful way to keep a secret. That is knowing the power of biblical thinking.

God wants to bless us with all His blessings. However, He will not waste His grace. He, as a wise Father, will not put into the hands of His children things that they will use for their destruction. With every heavenly privilege there is an earthly responsibility in its use. If God sees we are not going to take the responsibility, He will withhold the privilege. Moses learned this the hard way. In our fourth chapter, you remember, Moses wanted his own way. God let him have it, and as a result, he was not permitted to enter the Promised Land.

There is not only temporal value in biblical thinking, there is eternal value as well. As we daily obey the Lord, we give Him an opportunity to shower us with His blessings. This increases our faith in His Word and in Him. Then when the hour of our departure draws near, when we come to the end of our earthly journey, we need not fear. Knowing His Word, obeying His Word, trusting His Word, thinking thoroughly through His Word, we can take Him at His Word, that to be absent from the body is to be at home with Him. Thus, death will lose its terrors for us. We will not look forward to meeting the theoretical God of our lip service; we shall be looking forward to meeting our Heavenly Father whom we have learned to know through daily obedience to His Word.

Know the Living Word

It may be, friend reader, that some of you are good people, religious people. You know the Bible to be the world's best book, and you read it as excellent literature. You may have studied it for its precepts and as a religious guide for years. Could it be as you have read these pages you have given your assent to what has been written? Could it also be that you don't quite get it! It may be that you haven't received Christ Jesus as your own personal Saviour. This must be the first step in biblical thinking. Religion can be wonderful, however, it has one great drawback, it cannot give life.

Some time ago, I visited the mortuary in a certain city on behalf of one of my friends who was deceased. She had been a faithful member of our congregation. While waiting for the funeral director, I was scanning through some of his trade journals. One advertisement especially engaged my attention. It was promoting a certain cosmetic. Said the blurb, "Give your corpses that lifelike glow!'' I was somewhat surprised by the ad. When I went into the viewing room to see if everything was in order, I saw our friend laid out beautifully. She was handsome. She had on a gown she would never have worn in life. Painted fingernails were just coming in for the dead at that time, and hers were painted. As I looked at her the mortician had done his best for our friend. He only forgot to do one thing. He forgot to give her life. This is what the church does in religion. It dolls you up to go to heaven, but when it does not preach the Gospel it forgets to give you life in Christ so you can go there.

However, as you read these pages, you can take Him at His Word.

> Verily, verily, I say unto you, He that heareth my word, and believeth on him that sent me, hath everlasting life, and shall not come into condemnation, but is passed from death unto life. . . . For God so loved the world, that he gave his only begotten Son, that whosoever believeth in him should not perish, but have everlasting life. For God sent not his Son into the world to condemn the world; but that the world through him might be saved.
>
> John 5:24; 3:16,17

> I heard the voice of Jesus say,
> ''Come unto me and rest;
> Lay down, thou weary one, lay down
> Thy head upon my breast.''
> I came to Jesus as I was,
> Weary, and worn, and sad;
> I found in Him a resting-place,
> And He has made me glad.
>
> HORATIUS BONAR

14

The Purpose of Biblical Thinking

Now, IN OUR FINAL CHAPTER, we can ask the questions, "Is there power in biblical thinking for us? What should be the purpose of our biblical thinking? What should it do for us?"

In our studies in the previous chapters, the problems which the various characters taken from the Bible faced are somewhat like our own. Their methods of thinking are also closely related to ours. We, as they did, at times think positively, negatively, bitterly, uncertainly, lustfully, persistently, sensitively, arrogantly. Finally, we come into that joy of surrendered thinking when we rest in God's sovereignty. Our goal is to have the "mind of Christ" in all our daily experiences. In each of the studies we have found that when the men and women meant business with the Lord, there was a great change in their lives and they became victors of their circumstances. We have also noted how God's Word played a large part in their spiritual experience. In days of old, God spoke directly to His servants. In our day, we have His written Word, the Bible, and the ministry of the Holy Spirit to do for us what God did directly for them. To the degree that they were obedient to God's will there was blessing. The same can be true for us. To the degree that we study God's Word, to that degree will we master the art of biblical thinking and come to experience its power.

In writing to the Philippians, the apostle Paul gives us three great goals that we should reach in our mastery of biblical thinking: We should become joyful Christians, we should be Christians free from fear and anxiety, and we should possess minds devoid of bitter and nasty thoughts—thoughts which lead to bitter and unhealthy thinking. Paul gives us the marks of a healthy Christian mind which should govern our daily living.

Joyful in Spirit

"Rejoice in the Lord alway: and again I say, Rejoice" (Philippians 4:4). Again and again the apostle Paul sounds the word *joy* throughout this letter. One of the great ways a Christian can witness to his faith is by his joyful attitude in every circumstance. This *joy* Paul speaks of is not an artificial thing which is put on for effect. The *joy* of which he speaks is that joy born of God's grace. In the original language, *joy* and *grace* are cognate terms—terms related to one another. This is further emphasized when we see that the place of our rejoicing is to be in the Lord. Daily, as we meditate upon the goodness of God, we shall understand that we are the victims of His sovereign grace. Even when we experience a "blue Monday," we can rejoice that we are accepted in Him by His grace. On such a day our hearts can sing:

> 'In the Beloved' accepted am I,
> Risen, ascended, and seated on high;
> Saved from all sin thru His infinite grace,
> With the redeemed ones accorded a place.

> 'In the Beloved,' God's marvelous grace
> Calls me to dwell in this wonderful place;
> God sees my Saviour and then He sees me
> 'In the Beloved,' accepted and free.

MRS C. D. MARTIN

This joy, born of grace, is not a mere theological idea to the great apostle. He makes it very practical, as the next verse shows. "Let your moderation [reasonableness, fairness] be known unto all men. The Lord is at hand" (4:5). If we have been dealt with in grace, and we have, Paul then exhorts us to show that same grace to all men, whether they be of the household of faith or not. In our treatment of our fellows, especially in very negative situations, we too many times show the spirit of retaliation rather than the spirit of God's grace. As new men in Christ Jesus we are to give a heavenly response to a devilish stimulus. This is what grace demands of us.

It is interesting that Paul adds: "The Lord is at hand." Why? Paul always lived in the light of the Lord's nearing return. Not only would it be a time when he would see his Saviour face to face, but it would also be a time when his service for his Lord would be evaluated. He knew that he would stand before the judgment seat of Christ, not to be judged for salvation, but for his Christian witness and service (*see* 2 Corinthians 5:10). Part of that service which would be evaluated would be how the apostle treated others, on the basis of God's grace and not on what they might have deserved. Keeping this in mind, as did the apostle Paul, will cause us to make great changes in our reactions to people, especially those who are difficult to take.

Again, if we are truly filled with the Spirit, showing this kind of joy will not be difficult, since joy is a part of the fruit of the Spirit. We can save ourselves many ulcers if we know how to be joyful in horrid situations. Biblical thinking can enable us to reach this state of grace.

Anxious for Nothing

There are some passages in God's Word which at first reading do not make sense to me. Here is a case in point, "Be careful for nothing; but in everything by prayer and supplication with thanksgiving let your requests be made known unto God. And the peace of God, which passeth all understanding, shall keep your hearts and minds through Christ Jesus" (Philippians 4:6,7). Do you know what this text is saying? It is saying that you and I, dear reader, have no right, nor any grounds to be anxious or to worry. Do you believe it? Think of the many things about which you worry! Busi-

ness! Health! Children! Security! The future! "Be anxious for nothing. . . ." The Lord must be kidding. At least, Paul must be exag-
gerating! It does seem so in the light of all we could worry about.
A careful reading of the text and a thoughtful understanding of it
will show that Paul was dealing with a reality which we overlook.
In the first place, where does anxiety get us? Nowhere! Worry does
not help us in any situation; it only makes the problem worse. Furthermore, it is useless. I have a friend who is a great worrier. Her
husband, for example, will tell her that he will come home at a certain time. Foolishly she believes him. When 10:30 arrives and he is
not home, she begins to worry. At 11:00, she becomes concerned.
At 11:30 she wonders if the insurance has been paid. At midnight,
she is sure he has been killed. On one such occasion, at midnight
the police parked outside her house but did not come in. She saw
them through the living room window and was sure that they were
worrying about how to tell her the bad news, so she started worrying about them. At this moment in her anxiety, who should come
around the corner of the street and drive into the driveway but her
husband. Instead of feeling relieved, she could have killed him
because nothing had happened to him. Worry gets us nowhere.

In the second place, the apostle bids us pray with thanksgiving.
When we pause in our daily tasks to give thanks to God, it reminds
us what He has done for us. Since we are reminded that He cares
for us, it assures us that He is with us now as He was then. In our
prayers, Paul adds that we are to make our requests known unto
God. God would have us be specific in our prayers. We ought to
know what we want from Him. This may take some thinking, but if
we become specific in our prayers we are in the position of separat-
ing what we imagine from what is really the case. When we are ignorant of certain facts in a given situation, imagination takes over
and makes things worse than they really are. Furthermore, when we
pray in specific terms it gives us a chance to cool off from our
panic and emotional distress in order to accept the peace which God
is ready to give us.

In the third place, Paul suggests we make our request known

unto God. Why pray to God when our needs are here on earth? I may have bills to pay and the creditors are pressing me, or a person may need work. Why pray to the God of heaven? God may be in heaven, but distance is nothing to Him. As our heavenly Father, He is with us always. Furthermore, He knows the end from the beginning (*see* Isaiah 46:9,10). He knows the plans He has for us (*see* Jeremiah 29:11). We may not know the way we are to take, but He does (*see* Job 23:10). So instead of worrying, we can sing:

> Guide me, O Thou great Jehovah,
> Pilgrim through this barren land;
> I am weak, but Thou art mighty—
> Hold me with Thy pow'rful hand:
> Bread of heaven,
> Feed me till I want no more.

WILLIAM WILLIAMS
PETER WILLIAMS

Paul does not tell us that our burdens will be lighter if we pray to God. What he does tell us is that "the peace of God which passes all understanding" shall be our portion. Peace has the power to cool us off—settle us down—so we can think carefully and see our situation for what it is—not what we imagine it to be. Collecting our thoughts in the peace which God gives, we become victors of our circumstances instead of victims. Also, we embark on the adventure of working through our problems to a successful conclusion.

Think on These Things

The most important goal in the art of biblical thinking is that we may have a healthy mind in Christ. As we think, we are. If our thoughts are born of bitterness and retaliation we are a sick person. For the believer this is inexcusable. We can justify ourselves as we will, but God will not be impressed. He knows what He has given us in Christ to live for Him, and He expects us to use the provisions. Furthermore, we are to be the examples of healthy thinking to the world about us. Read the apostle as he writes:

> Finally, brethren, whatsoever things are true, whatsoever things are honest, whatsoever things are just, whatsoever things are pure, whatsoever things are lovely, whatsoever things are of good report; if there be any virtue, and if there be any praise, think on these things. Those things, which ye have both learned, and received, and heard, and seen in me, do: and the God of peace shall be with you.

> Philippians 4:8,9

Here the apostle gives us a blueprint of a healthy, Christian mind. He is telling us a number of things which we must take seriously: We are not to be liars, but men and women of integrity; we are to be men and women who are just in our dealings and not given to partiality in our dealings with others; we are to be clean in mind and body; we are not to run people down, nor are we to be carriers of gossip; we are not to make false virtues of our vices; we are to be known as people who praise the work of others and we are not to be miserable critics.

Verse nine may shock the brethren who always want to be nothing so the Lord can be everything. Paul never took this position. He wanted to be something in order to show that the death of Christ was not a total loss as far as he was concerned. He made it his business to walk worthy of his calling (*see* Ephesians 4:1). Thus he bids the Philippians to follow his example. At first thought we may feel this is arrogance on Paul's part, but careful consideration will lead us to see that it is not arrogance, it is the will of God to be carried out in each of us. For let us not forget that we are to be mistaken for our Lord (*see* Romans 8:29).

Conclusion

If we fully enter into the power of biblical thinking, we shall become a miracle people, having a healthy mind in Christ, being an example of our heavenly citizenship on earth, and continually and daily cleansed by His Word (*see* John 15:3). As we submit to the Word of God as we are led by His Spirit, the fruit of the Spirit will be manifested in our daily living (*see* Galatians 5:22,23). We shall become the kind of people that the world cannot do without. Nothing will be impossible for us. We shall walk in the footsteps of Paul, which leads to the Christ of victory. From wretchedness to restfulness we shall be "more than conquerors through Him who loves us." Paul's paean of praise will be our song of victory also.

O wretched man that I am! Who shall deliver me from the body of this death? I thank God through Jesus Christ our Lord. So then with the mind I myself serve the law of God; but with the flesh the law of sin. There is therefore now no condemnation to them which are in Christ Jesus, who walk not after the flesh, but after the Spirit. For the law of the Spirit of life in Christ Jesus hath made me free from the law of sin and death. For what the law could not do, in that it was weak through the flesh, God sending his own Son in the likeness of sinful flesh, and for sin, condemned sin in the flesh: That the righteousness of the law might be fulfilled in us, who walk not after the flesh but after the Spirit.

Romans 7:24–25; 8:1–4

Therefore:

And be not conformed to this world: but be ye transformed by the renewing of your mind, that ye may prove what is that good, and acceptable, and perfect, will of God.

Romans 12:2